So That

For Relationships

Jennifer Andersen Smith

Get the "So That" Journal *Free*!

When we go through hurdles in life, we can choose to use those lessons to help others "so that" their lessons are lighter. Now, Jen wants you to experience that same freedom of expression. The "So That" Journal is a guided workbook for exploring any life situation. It's a safe place to express your thoughts, feelings, hopes and dreams.

Go to www.jenniferandersensmith.com to download your bonus material.

Distribution by KDP Amazon and Ingram Spark (P.O.D.)
Printed in the United States of America and Canada

Title: So that
Names: Jennifer Andersen Smith – author
Website: www.jenniferandersensmith.com

Paperback ISBN: 979-8-9860436-0-9
Hardcover ISBN: 979-8-9860436-1-6
E-book ISBN: 979-8-9860436-2-3

Book description: When we go through hurdles in life, we can choose to use those lessons to help others "so that" their lessons are lighter. Using the "so that" principle, Jennifer shares her story of childhood trauma, teenage motherhood, and a loveless marriage in a compelling memoir that inspires her readers to step into their own power and take control of their lives.

Table of Contents

Dedication

This book is dedicated to all of you who heard part of my story and said "you should write a book".

I could not have completed this project without

The strength and wisdom of my God,

The absolute and infinite support of my husband,

The inspiration and encouragement of my kids,

The love and hope of my family and friends.

Love, Jen

The "So That" Principle

Introduction

When bad things happen to us, we are often tempted to ask, "Why did God let this happen to me?"

Challenges can seem like major tests of our faith, and we may wonder, "If there is a God, why did He allow this to take place?"

My life wasn't always a nice walk in the park. And I'm willing to bet yours wasn't either. Hardships come to all of us in various shapes and forms. Mine materialized in different ways throughout my life: childhood trauma, a bad 23-year marriage, struggles with depression.

So why do we have to live through these hardships? Instead of getting angry at God, I find it more constructive to look at things through the illuminating prism of the "so that" principle. Again and again, this principle has allowed me to heal my wounds and to process my trauma.

The "so that" principle is a twofold purpose for why you are here on this earth. It is 1) to learn and heal for yourself "so that" 2) you can pass on to others what you have learned. As we move through life, we all desire to find purpose. Having a purpose in life helps us to feel as though we matter and can make a difference. Without meaning or purpose, the suffering and pain in this life is so much deeper than we can ever hope to overcome alone in our humanity. However, God, in His infinite wisdom, has provided us with purpose in order for our human minds to make sense of the suffering and pain we experience.

The principle is found in verse 2 Corinthians 1:3-4 of the New Testament of the Bible.

Blessed be the God and Father of our Lord Jesus Christ, the Father of mercies and God of all comfort, who comforts us in all our affliction so that we will be able to comfort those who are in any affliction with the comfort with which we ourselves are comforted by God. 2 Corinthians 1: 3-4

Here, the Bible simply says that God shows us mercy and comfort in our pain "so that" we can pay that same comfort and mercy forward. We are commanded in this verse to share our comfort with others. As a part of sharing that comfort, we must also share our experiences and afflictions. We, as humans, are told to love one another and to comfort one another as God Himself has done.

Our life is temporary and, as such, we need to process the experiences we have pretty quickly. If we don't process our painful experiences adequately, we tend to develop bitterness or anger. On the flip side, if we don't process our joyful experiences properly, we stand to lose out on much of the joy those experiences could bring to us. These will also provide joy to carry us over the troubled times we will inevitably endure.

Knowing if you have processed your experiences enough is quite simple. Do you feel joy from positive experiences even though much time has passed? Has your pain eased, and has peace come forward in your feelings about negative experiences? Feelings of remorse signal that we need to forgive ourselves, while feelings of bitterness show we need to forgive another person. Are you able to provide comfort to another person in similar circumstances as you found yourself? Are you able to turn your experiences into teaching moments, not only for yourself, but also for those around you?

There's a saying "those who can, do and those who can't, teach". That saying has always bothered me. If you can do something, why wouldn't you not only do it, but then also teach it, pass it on? This is what parents do every single day, even if they don't mean to. Children first learn by simply mimicking those around them.

Next time you're with a baby, move your face in different expressions, the child will attempt (to the best of their ability) to make the same movements. Make noises to the child, the child will make the same noises back to you. This is foundational learning and sharing. This is the heart of God's commands to love and comfort one another in the way He loves and comforts us.

Remember, forgiveness does not mean we have let someone "get away" with their transgressions. Whether we are the transgressor or the transgressed upon, forgiveness means we can move forward in a productive way in our lives to face the next experience, and that we can do so without traces of the transgression continuing to color our feelings and decisions. Should we always show such compassion, caring, kindness just to risk being hurt again? Yes, but also no.

Forgiving someone does not mean you become a doormat and let this person run you over again and again. Forgiving someone means you no longer hold that transgression against them, but you can also arm yourself against the same behavior.

You, as a human, do not have the power to fundamentally change another human. You can only change your reaction. If you choose to see the good in someone, that's great, but if you choose to ignore the way they hurt you so that you can only see the good, that's not healthy for you in the long term.

Many years ago, I learned the "So that" principle through a wise and learned Sunday school teacher. She was in my life for a season of time and showed me how to learn what I needed. How to stay grounded in God's word and in my own self. She came into my life a few years before I finally acknowledged that my marriage was over. In so doing, what she showed me in the Bible and of our human experience was an intricate part of my processing the pain and sorrow I would feel as my marriage ended, as loved ones went through crises, as old friends fell away and new ones entered. As life changed so dramatically for me, I kept the phrase "so that" forward in my mind. I knew that God had a greater purpose in everything I experienced.

It's not that God gives or allows certain painful experiences to happen. God is an all-loving, all-knowing God who loves me and all His children deeply. You are a child of God whether you choose to accept His love and grace or not.

As a sign of that love, He gave us free will. This free will allows us to choose how closely we will align our lives with Him through prayer, Bible reading, and meditation. I'll be the first to admit, I have not always aligned myself closely.

At times, I have strayed so very far as to be unsure how to get back. The beauty of God is that even if you stray to the ends of the earth, He is always right there, inside your heart and walking beside you, ready to take your hand at your sincere, honest request. God is a benevolent God who suffers and is hurt at the painful experiences involved in our human experience. Especially those events that occur due to our actions against one another.

As the concept of this book came alive, and as I wrote it, I hoped it would help others understand the "so that" principle. I'm getting a bit ahead of myself so let's go back to the beginning and see how I got here.

Chapter 1

Beauty and Agony

"Allow beauty to rise from the pain"
- Jennifer

In the Beginning

My childhood was idyllic. I was raised on a small farm with many animals during the seventies and eighties. My parents were both raised on farms where their parents farmed the land, so it was natural for them to desire a larger homestead instead of an in-town lot. Growing up on the farm gave me freedom. The community around us was built around trust. My parents had no reason not to trust the neighbors. I used to go on a short bike ride into the nearby town in Illinois without any parental supervision. When it got really hot in the summer, my sister and I would go to the library because they had air conditioning. Then we would ride to the public pool and eat our lunch there while waiting for the pool to open at one o'clock. We would spend our afternoons swimming. Sometimes, Mom would pick us up and put our bikes in the trunk, which was always a huge treat at the end of a long day.

Both my parents worked full-time jobs outside the home and kept up a large garden and orchard and cared for various animals through the years. My father was a carpenter and ran a whole crew as the "Colonel". My mother was a school secretary. She got a second job in the eighties because interest rates were skyrocketing, houses weren't selling, and my dad didn't have enough work. Money was tight, but Dad expanded the family garden to have more food. Besides those occasional financial concerns, my parents created a beautiful life and family.

Every night, we gathered for family dinner. I was usually still dressed in the traditional Catholic school uniform of a plaid jumper and with knee socks. We all had our assigned seats. Mine was between my parents until my little sister came along. When she joined us at the table in her high chair, I was moved to a new spot, because she was little and needed more attention. Naturally, I was a tad jealous. Well, maybe more than a tad.

As much as a country girl can have a social life, I definitely did. I participated in Girl Scouts and softball teams. My friends would come for a sleepover, but I preferred to go to their houses in town. Their parents were usually more flexible about letting us go around town unattended.

My siblings and I were expected to go to church on Sundays and dress appropriately. No jeans or tennis shoes allowed, no t-shirts either. When we got older, we were allowed to go to later Mass, but we had to bring back a bulletin to prove we had gone. Such a silly thing really because we could have grabbed a bulletin on the way in and circled around and gone right back out. But that was the deal.

We had many different dogs and cats. Willie, Stephanie, Max, Trixie and Daisy were the dogs. The cats were mostly not named, but my little sister had one particular gray kitten called Mouse. Willie is the first pet I even vaguely remember. He was a chocolate lab but he ran away during the winter when I was 5. That would have been the winter of 1977. Even though I don't really remember Willie, I remember asking my mom where he went. I asked her if we could track him in the snow the next year when it snowed again. I guess my little 5-year-old brain thought the tracks would show up again in the next snowfall. I was hoping. Needless to say, Willie was never seen or heard from again.

It was my first time not having a concrete answer, and I was having a difficult time processing it. Many years later I asked my dad about him and his best guess was that he must have been hit by a vehicle on a road somewhere.

When it came to playing with the cats, mostly my sisters and I would annoy them by making them do tricks and keeping them in different boxes or cages while we played with them. But they were barn cats and not really pets; they had a job to do just like every animal on a farm. Their job was to keep the mice and other barnyard pests to a minimum in the barn and around the house.

Other animals we had through the years varied from horses to ducks to sheep to pigs to cows to chickens. Some of the animals were named Laverne, Shirley, Lenny and Squiggy, to name a few. We had a set of pigs once that were called Mike and Ike. Every proper farm needs a rooster so we had one too. His name was Chicken George and he was mean, vicious and angry. He actually came from my Uncle Joe, but I'm not sure if the chicken was a gift or a curse.

One sunny afternoon when I came home from school, I went into the barn to let Max the dog off his chain. Max was prone to running away during the day so we chained him in the barn in a way that he could get outside some and reach his food and water. But, as long as someone was home, he would stay home so we'd let him off the chain in the afternoon.

My brothers were home and I went to the barn to unhook him. But Chicken George was out in the main area of the barn and decided to mess with me. As I tried desperately to unhook Max, Chicken George kept fluttering into the way and scaring Max. Then Max would shy away and I would lose my grip. Max decided to fight back and chase the chicken. As he chased, he wound the chain around my legs. Mind you, my legs were bare because my Catholic school uniform was a dress, so the chain started to scrape and cut my skin. I yelled and yelled for my brothers to come help me.

Somehow, I finally got Max unhooked and unwound the chain from my legs. All the while I continued to holler for help. I finally made my way into the house and asked my brothers why they didn't come to help me, to rescue me. They said they never heard me. Then they said they did hear me, but they thought I was singing. Singing? What? Does my singing sound like hollering? At that moment, I don't know what upset me more: the pain in my legs or my brothers believing that my singing and hollering sounded the same.

Just because Max had hurt me didn't mean I was relieved from my duties. I still had to do my part to help the family because there are no days off on a farm.We were expected to help around the house for the girls; around the barn and yard for the boys. I was always jealous of that. Of course, who knows, I may have hated it. But, as it was, I wanted to be outside working with the plants and flowers. In the sunshine. However, every Saturday, we cleaned the house. My sister Rosie would usually offer to clean the bathroom.

We had one bathroom for all of us. The

bathroom was pretty big though. Probably measured 10' x 10' or more. I remember we each had our own drawer in the cabinet. Before my younger sister was born, mine was the bottom drawer because I was the youngest girl. I can still see my hair ties, ribbons and paraphernalia in there. Mom used Mary Kay for years. I can see her pink pots of potions she kept in her drawer. I would open the drawer and pull each pot out and read it just to see what they were.

As siblings we were expected to pitch in whenever something needed to be done. We didn't fight much from my perspective. But I know my brothers could be like oil and water. Just two very different people. I remember my dad and one of my brothers fighting a lot. This was largely because they were also two very different people. Looking back at it now, I can see they most likely were both super frustrated with each other.

I loved it when I got to do whatever I wanted. My sister Rosie and I did lots of performing on our driveway "stage". The driveway was elevated from the yard by about 2 or 3 feet, so it made the perfect platform. I would use the jump rope with one of the wooden handles as a microphone and put on concerts. Jump ropes and their handles make perfect microphones with wires. I often performed to my imaginary crowd. Mom and Dad didn't come sit for the performance. I don't remember ever finding Mom spying on me or anything. I felt free and alive as a child.

And then, my world got dark and claustrophobic.

Out of Eden

As a prepubescent, I was sexually abused by a boy six years older than me. He told me that he had learned about sex in health class and wanted to experiment. I was his guinea pig. I was about 8 years old when this started. I know this because the west room upstairs was still painted green and a toy room. Thus, it was not yet my older sister's room, which means my younger sister wasn't old enough yet to move upstairs. It is strange the details one remembers from these episodes.

He touched me in places no 8- or 9-year-old wants to be touched. He looked at me, as though inspecting me. I remember vividly one time in the hayloft. He would hold me down and breathe his milky smelling breath in my face. He would fondle my chest, which was completely flat, so I didn't get what he was doing. I wondered why he would do that. I remember feeling yucky after each encounter, but he always told me that was okay.

He began to taunt me with his actions. We would see each other on the bus and occasionally when he would find me out and about on my own. He wanted me to tell the other girls on the bus what he was doing to me. He threatened to do these same things to my sister and to the neighbor girls. I felt I had to protect them from this same ickiness that he brought whenever he was around. I definitely didn't want anyone else feeling this same way.

I knew what he was doing was wrong, but we didn't talk about things like this in my family. We were a good Catholic family who went to church each Sunday and followed the priest's teaching. How would I ever even come to my mom with this? Besides, when it wasn't happening, I put it out of my mind as quickly as possible. In all likelihood, I put my mind elsewhere even when it was happening.

I held this all inside for years and wondered what made me an easy target. Why me? Was it because I was the youngest girl in the neighborhood? Was it my naivete? I trusted him; he was a friend of our family. So why wouldn't I trust him?

He would be in our house or yard because he was friends with my brothers. He was completely trusted. No one had a reason to suspect anything. He groomed me well. I'm sure I had an infatuation with him at some point, although it makes me nauseous to think that now. But he was an older boy who would pay attention to me—who wouldn't like that? As a younger sister, and the youngest child for many years, I may have been a bit slighted on attention, or at least thought as much.

I know one time we were in the barn together. A usual occurrence. We were looking for the new kittens Dad had said were born. My sister and I loved playing with the kittens. However, we had to be very careful to not disturb them too much until they reached a certain level of maturity.

This boy and I climbed the ladder to the loft and then I crouched down looking in all the crevices for the nest of kittens. I don't know how the touching started, but it did and what I remember is lying on my back with his face over mine. His breath always smelled of stale milk. Not sour or bad milk, just stale, old milk.

I remember fearing pregnancy. He told me I couldn't get pregnant. He told me something about menstruation, but I didn't really get it then. I had not started. I do remember thinking in my bed late at night, that his actions meant I wouldn't be a virgin on my wedding day. Raised as a devoted Catholic girl, this was upsetting to me. I wanted to be that girl who saved herself for her husband. But he stole that from me. He stole my innocence. He stole my choices. The choice to be a virgin on my wedding night, the choice to enjoy sex as part of a loving, fulfilling marriage.

Chapter 2

Bloom Where You Are Planted

"Go back to that little girl inside you. Tell her all the ways you love her, believe her, value her."
- Jennifer

Family Meeting

Several years ago, on the advice of my therapist, I set up a meeting with my family to tell them about the abuse I suffered as a child. I asked my brother to host the meeting at his house rather than at my mom and dad's—where I grew up, where the abuse took place. It was a weekend afternoon in the fall. We all came together—Mom, Dad, brothers, sisters, spouses. No children, of course. I told my story. I read it directly from the pages I had written, which I still have.

When done, my brothers were beside themselves with fury. They could not believe that this person we all trusted, someone they had considered their friend, would do this to me. It further angered them to think of all the years they all lived in the same community, seeing each other at local events, stores, and restaurants. I had to plead with my brothers not to do anything to this person.

My brothers said I should report this, and my response was that I would not do that. I had dealt with it, this meeting being part of my process and therapy. They implored me to do so, to think of the others he might have done this to or future victims. While I would hate to think he continued that behavior, I had to put myself and my healing first. I had to be okay with my decisions. My decision was, and still is, not to report who the person was publicly.

I found out at this meeting that he did this to my sister. After finding that out, I wondered if he did it to the other neighbor girls because he had threatened to do exactly that.

Those who read this book from my hometown may be able to deduce who it is. Let those chips fall where they may. He has to live with what he has done to my sister and me. He has never sought forgiveness from me, and I have no desire to face him.

He still lives in the same town and by the

time I told my family about it, he was married with children. While I hoped and prayed he had not continued to prey upon young girls, I didn't have the emotional ability to take on that concern. I had to give that concern to God and trust Him to protect the girls near him.

I don't feel animosity or hatred towards him anymore. I just feel nothing. This was a thing he did to me, I wish he hadn't because it forever altered my life, but he did. He has to live with that shame and sin, not me. Maybe he is a Christian who has been washed of his sins. That's between him and the one true God. I cannot carry his shame.

I learned that bitterness and anger can control you even when you don't know it.

My sister has said she is not bitter, but her words have betrayed her. That day, during this meeting, she was very angry and bitter. Even though on that specific day she said she wasn't bitter. I tried to help her, but she was not in a place to listen as the pain was too much for her that day. I was not strong enough to help her. We have only spoken of it a couple of times since that day. When we do discuss it, I hear anger, resentment, heat, towards the person.

While I understand the reason and believe she is justified in her feelings, I wish she could find a way to resolve it for herself. I believe that some of this bitterness and resentment is the root of at least some of her health problems. Correlation between anger and illness has been made through research. I'm not certain that causation has been linked, but correlation certainly has.

Years ago, I watched a documentary called The Keepers about women who were abused in a Catholic girls' school as children and teens. One woman told her husband about it and she believes wholeheartedly that the reason he developed throat cancer, and subsequently died from it, is because he kept swallowing the rage and bitterness that he held towards the men who did it and the women who allowed it. She tearfully explained in the interview that she had begged him not to do anything or say anything as it would embarrass her. Her words left no doubt that she directly relates her request and his acquiescence to his throat cancer.

My first husband couldn't handle the full

truth of what happened once it all came out. He had thought it was much less serious than it really was. Of course, when I first told him about it, I was 16 or 17 years old, that good Catholic girl who didn't talk about sex or things of that nature. I most likely left a lot of holes for him to fill in as he imagined.

When I did finally tell him all of it, we had been living in Atlanta for a couple of years at least so that would put us at 32 or so. I had hoped he would have been equipped to handle it better. I do think that may have been the beginning of the end of our marriage. We tried more counseling since that time than ever before. Through the course of our 23-year marriage, we went to five marriage counselors.

This put up a big wall between us emotionally that neither of us could figure out how to get past. A couple of times after this, I felt suffocated during our intimacy. I know that freaked him out. I can't really blame him for that; I was freaked out too. But I needed compassion and understanding and, most importantly space. He did quite the opposite. In the last 10 years of our marriage, it was a constant battle for more sex. The harder he pushed, the farther away I pulled. I didn't want to give up that control, and he didn't understand what his actions were doing.

When I was a teen, Moonlighting was a popular show starring Cybill Shepherd and Bruce Willis. I loved that show. But Dad wasn't a big fan because they had sex on that show. And they were not married. He mentioned it once at the dinner table, which was very strange but looking back, I think that was his best attempt at the sex talk with his teen daughter that he was clearly concerned about. He just wasn't equipped with how to have that conversation.

As I sat there listening to Dad's voice his concerns, my thoughts were that it didn't matter anyway. I had already had pre-marital sex as an 8-year-old with the neighbor boy. It was too late for me. I was a bad kid, bad Catholic, bad person. Dad, I wish I could honestly say I never lied to you, but I know I did that day when I told you I wouldn't have pre-marital sex because I knew it was morally wrong.

Hindsight being 20/20, that would have been the perfect time for me to say, "Oh yeah, by the way, I'm not a virgin and the kid down the street, not my current boyfriend, is the reason why." But really, how could a naive girl say that to parents who didn't talk about these things? I don't remember having a conversation with my mom about my changing body even, let alone the next phase of physicality in my life after puberty—sex.

Just like my sister showed me where the makeup was and how to use it, she also showed me where the feminine products were kept and what to use.

This lack of conversation led me to be very open with my little sister about my pregnancy and the actions that led to it. We were driving into town shortly after my pregnancy had become known, just her and I in the car.

She asked me something about the baby and I used that opening. My older sister and I had both talked about making sure our little sister had that talk that we were never given. Later, I think that helped us have the hard conversations with our own kids.

Man, I can remember sitting in my daughter's room as she was a junior or senior in high school and talking about the ramifications of sex, physically and emotionally. But I was more focused on the physical part, and making sure to avoid disease and pregnancy.

Being Forgiving

This abuse affected me in multiple ways throughout my life. How would I say the "so that" principle was applied here? I learned how to forgive someone of a grievous transgression yet not let myself become a doormat through that process. Examples of that can be seen in the later years of my marriage and as I matured in my career.

Since I knew I couldn't be a virgin on my wedding night, I willfully participated in sex as a teen. While I don't know for certain I would not have done so if I had not been sexually molested, I also can't say for absolute I would have. I believe this led me into teenage pregnancy, because I had nothing to lose really. My virginity was stolen. As a child or teen, I did not understand the deeper essence of God's mercies and becoming new again through His divine grace. So I kept on, became pregnant at the age of 16, and had my first child at 17.

Don't get it twisted, I love my children 100%, and they know this. But I would not recommend teenage motherhood to anyone. I truly believe that because I have been close to my God throughout my life, He has continuously guided me as a parent. As such, I have four of the greatest kids a parent could ask for.

One of my goals as a mom was to have all my children graduate from high school without becoming parents first. I crushed that! Ha! All my kids graduated and were out of school for at least 5 years before blessing me with grandbabies. (Let me tell you, there really is nothing like being a grandma!) Have I made mistakes with them along the way? Absolutely. No doubt in my mind. But, through the Grace of God, they are all fantastic, productive, self-sufficient adults.

My curiosity about sexual acts is borne mostly from this abuse. I believe I've spent times in my life trying to find out what the bigger part of sex is all about rather than seeing it through the lens of the abuse. Surely it must be more than just this physical act. I do know there is power and vulnerability in action. I have never been a big fan of sex. I don't doubt that it is due to the initial experiences I had with the act. He didn't know anything radical or kinky, but I knew what he was doing wasn't morally right, even as a child.

I learned how to understand that everyone has their own healing process and pace. My own sister has dealt very bitterly with this experience. While I cannot blame her for feeling that way, I can certainly wish better for her. I pray that she now feels peace by understanding the "so that" principle herself and learning to move forward. I can also take the time to truly understand, appreciate and validate my own feelings about this experience in order to be what she needs when it comes to discussing this situation, or not discussing it. That's love really. To be what others need us to be but still be honest and true. It's a fine line between becoming what they need us to be and staying honest in ourselves.

Many years ago, I received a phone call I had prayed I would never receive. A very close friend of mine has a daughter who was about

6 or 7 years old and she had been preyed upon by a deviant person. This girl's older brother, probably only 12 or so himself, had decided to use her to experiment with his sexuality. Much in the same way I was used. For years, this darling girl suffered from many side effects of fear, misplaced shame, and insecurity.

I remember immediately going to be with them as I felt I could maybe help in some way, just by understanding how their little girl might be feeling. As it turned out, I was just sitting silently with her dad and he asked me, "Jen, I just don't know what to do. What can I do?"

I held his hand, looked him in the eye, and quietly said, "Keep her safe. She needs to know that Daddy will always be here to keep her safe, to hold her whenever she needs it, to comfort her whenever she is scared."

Daddies are very powerful emotionally for their daughters, and most men don't realize that. They are busy in the day-to-day of providing for their families and the minutiae of just getting things done. But, dads, the most powerful, restorative, loving thing you can do for your girls is to hold them and tell them in words and actions that they are safe and loved.

While in the midst of writing this book, I received another phone call that I absolutely hate to have received. More so, I hate that such a call had to be made by this sweet young woman. This kind, compassionate young woman called because she was recently assaulted by a young man she thought was her friend. She went to his house to hang out, which was a usual occurrence, and he proceeded to try to rape her. Thank God in Heaven that she was able to get out of there before it was completed. But, as is understandable, the situation completely traumatized her.

However, because of my experience, I feel that I was better equipped to handle the phone call than if I had not had my own experience. I feel I could advise her better on her options and what her next steps should be than if I had not had my experience. Would I trade my experience and get rid of it from my life if I could? Absolutely, yes, in so many ways, but then I look at how I helped these loved ones and wonder, would I trade it out and not be able to help them? I don't know that I would, I just don't.

This is how the "so that" principle works. Because of my experience and processing it through my faith in God and the comfort He has provided, I can share God's comfort with others. And for that, I thank God.

Chapter 3
Choices and Consequences
"Choices are the hinges of destiny."
- Edwin Markham

Dating Teens

It was a lazy Saturday afternoon at the end of September during my junior year of high school. My parents were gone for the day; in fact, no one was home. I decided to take a nap because what else should teenagers do when left to their own devices? I took my current book and snuggled into Mom and Dad's bed with their satin comforter—so comfy.

About an hour later I was awakened by the phone ringing. Not a cell phone like we would have now, a rotary dial desk phone with very little control of the ringer volume. Since it was in the room with me, it startled me awake. Back then, you had to answer the phone to know who was on the other end. It was my best friend, Bobbi. She had just been on the phone with a mutual friend, Chris. He wanted to know if I wanted to date his friend Brent.

Well, my initial thought was something like, "Why didn't he call me himself?" So, I said no. He needed to call me if he wanted to go out with me. After discussing further to be sure that's the answer I wanted to give, Bobbi hung up to call Chris back. What you don't know is that I'd had my eye on this guy for a bit now. I went with him and Chris to a couple of different football games and did some flirting in the classes we shared.

As my sleepy mind woke up, these thoughts became clearer to me and I called Bobbi back in a quick panic. I told her to call Chris back and tell him I had changed my mind. She laughed and said she would call him back and tell him to have Brent call me himself.

When he called, he told me he hadn't called himself because he was nervous to call me at first for fear of rejection. I thought that was sweet. I told him I had been woken out of a sound sleep, and that's why I said no initially. He laughed at that.

Our conversation was cut short because he had to go to work. He was a delivery guy at

Joey's Pizza, the best pizza in our hometown. There was even a time or two I went with him for deliveries until curfew. Since I was still 15 and not allowed to date until I was 16, we had to do group dates for a few weeks. Chris rode along with us to make it a group. Such a good friend.

We had many adventures together. We went to many football games and then ate at Wolfenberger's after. At the beginning of our senior year, we had some friends who had graduated and got their own places the year before. We had parties at their apartments. The first time I got drunk was at one such party. Bartles & Jayme's wine coolers were easy to drink. Sweet, smooth, and delicious. I didn't realize how much alcohol I'd had until I tried to stand up. At least, I didn't know that night.

Oh wow, it was time to head home for curfew, but my head was spinning so bad, and Brent was in no condition to drive. Thank goodness our friend Chris was around. He took me to a phone booth (no cells, remember?) so I could call home and make some excuse to stay out later. I was so anxious about being caught by the way I talked on the phone. Somehow, I controlled my slurring and got the permission I needed.

We would go bowling at Four Seasons and play pool too. Often a friend would host a bonfire so we'd hang out there all night. Snowmobiling was another winter favorite activity.

We had agriculture class together. I also took a horticulture class, so my agriculture projects were usually of flowers and plants. We were both in the FFA (Future Farmers of America) club at school. We both did dairy judging contests for a few years. We went on ski trips with the FFA group and just with friends. In our junior year, we were both officers. Then, in our senior year, we were voted as President and Vice-President, so that was cool.

Well, until it became known that I was pregnant.

Brent and I were worried for quite a while that I might be pregnant, but we had convinced ourselves that ignoring the issue would make it go away. Yeah, not so much. In November of our senior year, Mom started noticing that my clothes weren't fitting as well. She was always looking out for me, and she was such a good mom with her unconditional love.

As the soft morning light filtered through my curtains, one early Saturday morning, Mom came to my room. She quietly sat down on my bed and gently shook me awake. I was so confused. Mom never came upstairs unless she absolutely had to. Even if she did come up, it wasn't to wake us. She could do that by calling from the bottom of the stairs.

Once I cleared my head and sat up in bed, she asked, gently and quietly, "Are you pregnant?" I immediately broke down in tears and admitted it. I had been holding that back for so long. It was truly a relief to talk to Mom about it. Of course, she was highly disappointed in me, but she also made me feel like it wasn't the end of the world. Now we had to start talking about care, options, future plans.

One night, we met at my house to discuss the situation with Brent's parents. I remember his dad being there but I don't remember his mom being there. I'm sure she was, but I just don't remember her. We discussed the options available with the pregnancy. The future plans that Brent and I may have had were now altered. Certain options were off the table completely while other options were now reviewed.

During this meeting, and in conversation with Brent and my own prayer time, I decided I had to give the baby up for adoption. What was a 17-year-old kid gonna do to raise a baby on her own? I could just see a life of want and need in front of us both. This also changed my dream of being an architect. I had already been applying to colleges but now, those seemed to be far-off, unattainable dreams. Unless I gave up the baby. Surely we could find a wonderful family to love him or her and give the baby a beautiful life.

At this time, I was still in Girl Scouts and trying to get my Gold Award. We had a small troop, only 3 or 4 of us. Bobbi was in the troop with me, we had been friends and in scouting together since elementary school. During a meeting, we discussed what I was going to do about the baby. I told them all we were going to give the baby up for adoption. My scout leader asked me if that was something I really thought I could do. I admitted, for the first time, it was not. How could I live not knowing anything about this child and where he or she might be, what they were doing, how they felt? I was very unsettled with this decision now that I had had it questioned. For me, family has always been a very important part of my life. I'm a very traditional person with traditional values and upbringing.

After bringing it up with Brent, he was relieved. He did not want me to give the baby up, but also felt like he didn't really have the final say. He suggested we talk with his mom. She had given up a child around the same age in her life. Maybe she would have some insight. After talking with her about her experience, I knew I couldn't do it. The trick was having this conversation with my folks now and getting their support.

I think they were relieved too. This was their first grandchild and I don't think they really wanted to have him or her adopted away from the family. They were so incredibly supportive. They agreed to help raise the child until we could be out on our own. We moved things around in my room so we could make room for a crib. We decided to redecorate it, new paint, curtains, etc. The night I went into labor, I had to pull the protective plastic sheeting off my bed before I could go to bed. But, by the time I got home a few days later, it was all ready to go.

Brent was even allowed to stay at my house, sleeping on the couch, for the first few weeks after the baby was born. It was pretty helpful to have another person there. I was so not prepared to be a mom. Looking back now, at the age of 47 with 9 adult children and step-children and 9 grandchildren of my own, I realize just how completely unprepared I was to be a mom. I am so grateful that God provided all that He did to help me and the babies get through their child-hoods with beautiful outcomes. In the end, the decision to keep the baby was the right one for us.

Within just a few months of the birth of my first child, I found out I was pregnant with child number two, Norah. So, I was going to be a mom again and I hadn't even turned 18 yet. This was definitely not in my plan, but my actions led directly to it.

Why in the world did I end up pregnant

again? Well, there is the obvious answer, the one my dad and brothers like to joke about. But it goes deeper than the physical actions. There was emotion and immaturity in the choices, or rather a lack of active choices. I had just had a baby at 17, two months before I graduated from high school. I was still a teenager. I was still capable of making decisions that affected my future in ways I didn't consider because I was still a teenager. So I tried to be smart and I went on the pill.

After just 6 weeks, I was convinced by an older and wiser person (or so I thought) that I shouldn't be on birth control. Looking back, I think he was really trying to convince me to abstain from sex, but I didn't grasp that at the time and just stopped taking the pill. And poof, I was pregnant again.

Chapter 4

Accepting the Consequences

"When you make a choice, you also choose a consequence". - Jennifer

Looking back on my choices during this time, I come back to the same decision point. At least, the one about sex. I still believe that if I had not been sexually abused, I would not have made the same choices about sex as a teenager. I had the meaning of sex all twisted in my head.

I thought sex was needed in a relationship to hold on to my partner. I felt that if I didn't "put out," he would lose interest in me and find someone else. As a not particularly popular teenager, I really didn't want to not have a boyfriend. Frankly, many teenagers put too much pressure on themselves and their classmates regarding relationships.

Maybe I would have made better choices with more conversation about relationships and what makes them work well versus what doesn't. But, that just wasn't how my parents chose to approach the subjects. Instead, they gave us rules about what we couldn't or shouldn't do but not really what we could or should do. Maybe I would have made different choices.

The world will never know, though, will it? I made these choices and I lived the life that these decisions created.

Frankly, I don't regret it.

I don't wish for a "do-over". On the contrary, I believe that the bad parts make the good parts that much more valuable to us. The good parts shine brighter with hope because of the bad. The fun and adventurous parts of life are more exciting, funnier, and happier because we know that life can be so dark, scary, and lonely.

Impulsivity created these situations, which then required quick decision making. Have you ever looked back to the outcomes of decisions you made quickly versus the ones you took time to learn more about and then decide? I have. For me, by just looking at the outcome, I can tell you if the decision was made quickly or if time and consideration were used first.

In my experience, making impulsive decisions doesn't work out nearly as well as taking your time. Think about it for yourself. Maybe you are the opposite of me. Maybe you know how to make quick good decisions and make them well. It doesn't seem to matter if the situation is a big, impactful one or just something simple.

For example, when I have made quick paint color choices, I typically end up painting the room twice because that first one is not pretty. A few years ago, we were painting the bedrooms and I was pushed to make a quick choice. I thought a soft green would be very pretty. Unfortunately, I wasn't allowed the time to truly think this through and chose a color reminiscent of institutions in the 1950s. Not exactly warm and welcoming. I had more time to choose a color for the second bedroom and picked a warm peach shade. I still love that color years later. Unfortunately, the first bedroom had to be painted again with a nice blue color before we liked it.

This example is just a minor inconvenience. The financial costs were minimal, the time commitment was small. But it's a good example of how making impulsive and unresearched decisions can affect you in multiple ways.

The decision to have sex when I did while only 16 years old was a decision I made impulsively at the moment. The Bible tells us that "the Spirit is willing, but the flesh is weak." That was true for me. I succumbed to the desire of my physical body and made a snap decision that ended up affecting the trajectory of my life.

Chapter 5
Promises Kept, Promises Broken
"I felt so much that I started to feel nothing."
- Unknown

First Mother's Day

My first child, Tony, was born in March of my senior year. As the weeks went by, we found our footing with this baby thing. I had decided not to nurse because, well, I was a 17-year-old girl. But I was still at home for several weeks on maternity leave from my senior year in high school. I was missing out on the last few weeks of schooling, missing my friends, missing the challenge of school. It was difficult because I didn't feel like me anymore, even though my brother and his wife had made it quite clear to me that just because I was having a baby, that didn't change who I was as a person. The person at my core was still me, no matter what. But when you're stuck at home with a newborn and a tutor, it begins to feel like everything has changed. I began to look forward to any social activity. Even a simple dinner out, just to get out of the house.

My very first Mother's Day was quickly approaching. I happily anticipated the day even though no 17-year-old girl thinks it will be to celebrate her entry into motherhood but to celebrate her own mother and grandmothers. Brent began to tease me about the great Mother's Day gifts I would get. He would talk to our baby and tell him not to tell, to keep the secret. I began to really get excited about the day. I love presents and being celebrated, and this sounded like it would be a second birthday each year. What could possibly be wrong with that, right?

That morning I woke up with great excitement, ready to celebrate my mom and grandmas but also to be celebrated too. As per usual for a Sunday, we started our day by going to church with Mom and Dad. I do believe that some of my siblings would have come along. After church, we went back to Mom and Dad's to have a family celebration. I still lived at home. Brent, my siblings, Grandma, and Grandpa all came over to celebrate a beautiful spring day.

We all had brunch together and gave Mom

her cards, flowers, and gifts. This year, my siblings and I gave our mom a custom ring we all bought together. She still wears it today. We were all so excited to do this for her. My siblings and I had a Mother's ring custom designed with all our birthstones. Mom loved it. Watching her excitement built mine up too!

I thought it a bit odd that Brent did not give me any presents or cards at that time, but I brushed it off, thinking he wanted privacy or something. We left Mom and Dad's to go to his mom's, and still nothing. We visited with his mom for a bit, and then he brought me back home.

I remember feeling shocked that he still had not brought a Mother's Day gift for me. What was happening? I hadn't even got so much as a "Happy Mother's Day" greeting from him, let alone a card, flowers, or the simplest of gifts. Of course, being so shocked, I didn't process it at all, but I do vividly remember being stunned that he could be so indifferent and quite frankly a bit of a liar.

I wanted to give him the benefit of the doubt, so I talked with him about it. I reminded him of the teasing he had done through our son and directly with me, which heightened my excitement. But, he really had nothing to say. He didn't think he had done anything terrible and didn't think he should apologize for anything. He just didn't get it.

Looking back now, I think I was probably dealing with depression even then. It's common for women to struggle with some depression after the birth of a child. While I know I didn't struggle with a serious case of this, I do know I had difficulty adjusting to being a mom. There were days I absolutely could not stand it when the baby cried. Other days I could tolerate it well enough.

I felt good about my ability to take care of him physically - to meet his basic needs for food, clothing and shelter. What overwhelmed me was the thought of raising a child. The actual thought of teaching him how to be a good person scared me.

Also, looking at my body, I was not proud of it. I had gained more than 50 pounds during the pregnancy. At barely six weeks out, I had only lost a little weight. I didn't know how and it wasn't a focus. I had never had to worry about losing weight or improving my physical fitness before. It was all-natural to me. I was a busy teen with a lot of activity to burn off any junk food I indulged in.

When I had taken Tony to his first couple of doctor's appointments, I remember feeling like an imposter when I walked out of the office. The doctor I had chosen for Tony was a family friend, someone my mom saw personally for years. I thought it made sense to choose a doctor who knew us. I thought that would mean the doctor wouldn't look down on me as a very young mom.

I was wrong. I don't know if he intentionally talked to me condescendingly, but it happened. He made me feel inferior as a mom. I just did not know what to do. This added to my doubt and apprehension of my own abilities to be a good mom.

Having a gift to mark my first Mother's Day may have built up some self-confidence as a mom, especially a very young one. A gift would have been a symbol of appreciation and assurance from someone else that I was doing the right things as a mom.

South Cross Apartment

We moved into our very first apartment in August of 1989. It was on South Cross Street in Sycamore. The rent was government-subsidized and cost maybe $444 per month for us. It was a lot for two kids fresh out of high school and only one full-time job, a baby, and another on the way. But, along with the help of my family, we managed it.

The apartment was on the ground floor with two bedrooms, one bath, and a ginormous master closet. We considered using it as a nursery for the new baby since the second bedroom was pretty small. There was a communal laundry room in the building's hallway. A sweet older lady lived across the hall. Our upstairs neighbors liked to vacuum at 2 am and weird times like that. Luckily, Tony didn't wake up for that.

We were pretty happy there. We had three different couches during that time. One was an ugly rust-orange couch with rough fabric, the next one was a cute floral couch that I loved. My mother-in-law bought it for us from Goodwill for my birthday. The last one was a blue set we bought from my uncle's auction. It was a brand new couch and loveseat that lasted us for many years. It's so exciting to get brand new furniture. As an 18-year-old, I felt very adult making that purchase.

Six months after moving into our apartment, we welcomed our second child. This time we had a sweet little girl and named her Norah. Norah was born exactly 375 days after Tony. My very own Irish twins.

Brent had begun to develop a good relationship with his father John through Tony's existence. Something about that third generation began to form a bond, a common interest finally between father and son. Before Tony's birth, John was never really involved in Brent's life. He was 45 years older than Brent, a part of a completely different generation, and he had left the raising of the kids largely to their mother. John was a good man with his own faults, just like each of us. He worked hard and kept to himself, but there was always great love for his family. Brent has that same great love for his family. He inherited that from both of his parents and it was a big part of what kept us together as a couple for so long.

During that time, Brent worked as a mechanic for DelMonte. June was the midst of the harvest season which typically ran from the middle of May through the month of October. When it was harvest season, Brent would often get no more than 1 day off per month.

One beautiful June evening, my future father-in-law showed up unexpectedly at our apartment. I had started working on a little dinner for myself and Tony while he played in the living room. John unexpectedly appeared over the railing of the patio to our apartment. He called hello to Tony through the open patio door and I invited him in. John played with Tony and held Norah, and we all had a simple dinner while enjoying each other's company. This was on a Sunday night, and we had no idea that it would be the last time we would see him.

Just a day or two later, John went to work that morning like he had every morning for many years. He was the courier for a global corporation based in our hometown. His job was to drive the van from the company campus to the post office, airport and everywhere in between. Whatever needed to be picked up, whether person or parcel, and delivered elsewhere, was his responsibility. He truly enjoyed his job. He had a plan to retire soon and buy an RV. He was so excited about that idea, as excited as an extreme introvert will show you anyway.

When John got to work, he ran his usual errands and then was called into his boss's office. He went readily assuming it was just another task for his list. However, it was completely the opposite. He was let go. The company stated it was because they were concerned with his driving record and his ability to continue to drive safely for them. In the previous quarter, he had apparently been in a couple of small scrapes, no major damage and no injuries. John was so upset by this news that he refused a ride home, took his belongings and started walking.

That day was very warm and very humid for a June day. I had just taken the babies for a walk in the stroller and was drenched with sweat and humidity. While trying to unlock the apartment door, I could hear the phone ringing. This was a wall phone, way before cell phones were so popular. I left the kids in the stroller in the hallway while I rushed in to grab the call. It was Brent telling me the terrible news.

Apparently, when John was walking home, he suffered a heart attack and fell in the ditch. He was not found until later that afternoon when the factory next to his former employer had their shift change. One of the factory workers saw him lying there and tried to help, but it was already too late.

If Brent had had more time with his father to solidify that relationship, I believe Brent would have been a different, emotionally stronger person. As it was, he now had twice been stunted in his attempts to develop a relationship with his dad. Once, when he was about 9 and his parents split up, and now, at the vulnerable time of being a new dad himself.

Getting Married

The day of my wedding was crazy hectic. Not at all what I thought it would be like. Every girl thinks about her wedding day to a certain extent. I really thought it would be more relaxing and calm.

My children were blessed to have a second mom, whom they call JuJu to this day. She is Brent's cousin, and I remain close to her and consider her another sister. On our wedding day, JuJu cared for Tony and Norah. She met us out at Mom and Dad's in the morning, and I didn't have another worry about them all day. After passing off the kids, I picked up my dress, and we all headed to the church and school. We used the kindergarten classroom of the elementary school as the place to get ready. It so happened to have been my kindergarten classroom 15 years earlier.

My aunt Roxie met us at the school to do my hair. She made it all curls cascading down one side. I loved that hairstyle. I still love that I chose that style. Aunt Rox made it look so good too. Rosie, Teddy, Grandma Herrmann, and Aunt Roxie all gathered with us.

I put my dress on. I don't remember this being a moment or having pics done during this time. At some point, I went into the bathroom in the teacher's lounge to do my makeup. I was alone. I remember it being very quiet.

The light in the lounge was off so it was a

little dark. The light was off near the front desk and entrance to the school. The only light was that of the November sun shining. It was a bit weak if I remember correctly, a winter sun.

I was nervous, scared. I would label the feeling as anxiety now—almost an out-of-body feeling. I can see myself in the bathroom doing my makeup with my little stash of Maybelline eye shadow and mascara. I'm pretty sure I did not use foundation or blusher at that time in my life. Just some eye shadow, mascara, and maybe lip color of some sort.

As I watched myself get ready, I could feel this sense of dread creeping in, not so much the anxiety now. Anxiety implies more energy than I felt. My thoughts were quiet. Calm, steady. I would like to think that if someone had come to me at that moment and asked me if I was 100% absolutely certain to go through with this wedding, I would have said no. I don't love him enough to marry him for life, I thought. I like the idea of marriage. The traditional family setting of marriage, but really, I don't love him that much.

Looking back, I'm not sure I ever felt

true love for him as a wife, lover or life partner should. At first, I mostly felt infatuated and was in love with the idea of being in love. Many teenage girls feel the same way, but they don't get themselves in quite the same situation, so it doesn't impact the trajectory of their lives as completely.

I also felt a sense of responsibility for these children we created together. I had agreed to raise them when I couldn't go through with adoption. I have always held a very traditional set of values. Raising a child means Mom and Dad are there, together.

So I got married.

After the wedding ceremony and millions of pictures, we had planned to drive ourselves to the reception in our fancy new Pontiac 6000 sedan. As we left the church, light snow was falling. We were alone except for our best man and then realized none of us had the car keys! My purse had been picked up by my bridesmaids or parents and taken to the reception hall to be helpful. Brent did not have keys on him for some reason and neither did Chris, our best man.

I can't remember exactly how we got ahold of anyone, but I'm sure it had to be before they got to Genoa for the reception because it didn't seem to be that long. This, of course, was long before everyone had a cell phone in their pocket. Eventually, we got a key and made our way to the Vets hall in Genoa for the reception.

We had a full dinner downstairs in the Vets Club. I don't know what we ate. The kids sat at a table with JuJu, right in front of us. There were the requisite toasts, merriment and family time. Before we ate, we cut the cake and fed each other. I think it must have been rather uneventful since I don't remember it.

Eventually, we made our way upstairs for the dancing. My brothers supplied my new husband with plenty of drinks even though we were underage. He was hammered pretty early on. Tried to dance with me in a way that made me feel awkward. I felt his dancing was too sexual and it felt embarrassing. Looking back, I think he just doesn't know how to dance any other way.

We tossed the bouquet and garter. Next was the dollar dance. I was excited about this because each person had to pay a dollar to dance with the bride or groom. Typically the best man and maid of honor would hold the money and keep the line moving. I'm sure we walked away with a few hundred dollars from that, but I don't remember ever seeing it.

By the time we got ready to leave, Brent was completely drunk, and I'd not had a drop of alcohol. Maybe if I'd had, it would have been more fun for me.

As it was, I was now experiencing new anxiety because I knew nothing about our honeymoon plans. I had been fine with that because I handled all the wedding items myself. It was the only thing I asked him to take care of other than his own tux and his groomsmen.

The Honeymoon

We had a town car pick us up. Brent stumbled in the back and promptly fell asleep. Luckily the driver knew to take us to O'Hare. We flew the red-eye flight to Vegas. It was a good thing I had stuck with my usual traveling plans and brought a book. I read my book the whole flight while he slept stretched out across the aisle, oblivious to anyone needing to get up or down it. Back in 1990, flights could be nearly empty but would still fly. This flight had maybe a handful of people. No one was around us.

We landed in Vegas, and I had to wake up my new husband from his drunken sleep. He finally awoke enough to tell me we were heading to our sister-in-law's in San Diego at Camp Pendleton. Yippee! I was so excited to see her and my niece and nephew. I hadn't seen them for some time. Bree and I would write long letters to each other to help get through whatever perilous phase our children were currently in. It was a real treat when our husbands would talk to each other on the phone so we could then do the same. This was back when long distance was expensive. The idea of spending a week there was very exciting. I had also never been to California or the west coast.

My darling husband slept on the second flight as well. We finally got into California, and to our hotel for the night around 2 am California time. I had been up for nearly 24 hours straight. But it was our wedding night, and I wanted to make it special. At my bachelorette party, a friend had given me an absolutely gorgeous emerald green gown with black lace—very sexy. The sexiest thing I owned, ever. I went into the bathroom to get ready. And, you guessed it, when I came out, he was sound asleep with no hope of being awakened. Out came my book once again.

We headed over to Bree's the next morning and enjoyed a day with them. Saw their townhouse, played with the kids, did a little sightseeing. Bree recommended we go to the Hungry Hunter restaurant or something like that. Brent and I went and enjoyed it greatly. Delicious food, yummy bread. Unfortunately, Brent's brother was in Japan doing a year overseas, so we could not spend time with him.

The second day we took the trolley to Mexico. That was an adventure and a half! Some of Bree's friends came too. I think the trolley ride took about an hour. When we crossed the border, they warned us to ignore the beggars and the people who confronted you to buy their wares.

I was not prepared for the sight of so many people sitting on the curb begging. I was a country farm girl from the Midwest who wasn't used to seeing homeless people or panhandlers in the city, let alone seeing them in a different country and looking so incredibly poor. Their lack of decent clothing and shoes was striking. There were so many children. This was different from the beggars in Chicago, who are grown adults, typically men. The worst thing about their appearance is typically their teeth or hair looking unkempt.

We moved quickly through the streets to the market we were heading for. We did a little shopping but mostly just strolled through the market. We visited a rooftop bar where they gave us tequila shots and delicious margaritas. I don't remember doing the shots, but I certainly drank my share of margaritas.

I remember buying an outfit of a pair of shorts and a tank top. We also bought a blanket. Both items were very scratchy. I brought them home and washed them several times to soften them. We bought gifts for the kids, a set of maracas I still have. Gifts for Teddy and JuJu who were the primary caregivers for our kids while we were gone.

Upon our arrival back at home, we settled back into our life together. As you will see in the passages to come, there are moments of beauty and joy and moments of confusion, sadness, and hurt. As I look back on my life, I choose to remember the moments of beauty and joy as opposed to focusing on the harder parts. There are lessons in all the moments if we are looking for them.

Chapter 6
Becoming Aware

"I am learning a new way to think so that I can learn a new way to be." - Jennifer

I didn't realize it at the time, but these early experiences taught me to doubt and mistrust my husband. It was so subtle that I didn't realize that I did not trust him for many years.

Ruth Bell Graham is quoted as saying, "A good marriage is the union of two forgivers." Our marriage was the union of two competitors. We were two people who didn't fully believe in or trust ourselves, let alone each other. We competed against each other for who was right when decisions had to be made.

In the early days, I thought I was in love, and that love could overcome any concerns, any issues, any worries. Now I know that to be untrue. Love can certainly overcome a lot of issues. But, if you have that love without trust, is it true love? I say no, it is not.

The "so that" principle that this book is based on, is found in 2 Corinthians. But, if we look at one book before that in the Bible, we find a beautiful description of what true love is.

Love is patient, love is kind. It does not envy, it does not boast, it is not proud. It does not dishonor others, it is not self-seeking, it is not easily angered, it keeps no record of wrongs. Love does not delight in but rejoices with the truth. It always protects, always trusts, always hopes, always perseveres. Love never fails. 1 Corinthians 13:4-8 NIV

Did you notice the fourth to last item? Love always trusts. God doesn't tell us that sometimes love means trust in your lover and sometimes it doesn't. Love Always Trusts. Without trust, love cannot remain.

There have been times in my life that I have not trusted the Lord but thought I loved Him. Without trust, love means very little because you cannot grow together. The kindness and patience of love is diminished, the tolerance of love is destroyed when trust is not present.

Creating trust requires full disclosure and clear communication between the parties. When we share our needs with our partners in the trust-building process, we expect those needs to be respected and protected. But, if our partner exploits those needs or makes fun of them or makes fun of you for having them, the trust is broken.

So many of the lessons I learned through the first 18 years of my life were not intentionally part of in my decision-making until much later in life. Getting married at the tender age of 19, being a mom of two at that time, and trying to figure out everything that meant, left me with little time to sort through my thoughts. At the time, it was everything I could do to get through each day, as any mom of little ones will tell you.

Self-care is vital. I did none. When I became a mom and wife, I threw everything I had into it. I had been taught how to cook, I knew how to care for the babies, I could clean, do laundry, manage money. All the things I thought I should do. I was motivated to be the best I could for my children. I will be the first to admit that the focus should have been on my husband AND on my children, but it was easier to focus on the kids and their needs, so that's what I did.

Through the years, by focusing on my children over my husband, the chasm between us widened to a point of no return. I never attempted to cross that expanse, not truly anyway. By the time I recognized a problem, our relationship was already crumbling and falling apart.

I know now, over 25 years later, that I didn't trust Brent fully and completely during our marriage. Even before the wedding, to be honest. There was a time when I was out of town on a Girl Scout trip when we were seniors that I found out he went out with another girl. And then there was a time when I was pregnant that we got into an argument at my house and he stormed out of there angry and drove his car insanely down Mt. Hunger road as I watched him. I feared he would hurt himself or possibly never come back. As a 16- or 17-year-old girl, it's scary to have that happen. If he hadn't come back, it might have been for the best.

That was when I started to take a serious look at my relationship and contemplate its future. I would recommend that you not be as naive as I was. I would recommend that you take stock of your relationships regularly.

Take some time to assess your relationships in all areas of life. Look at your connections with your partner, children, parents, siblings, and close friends. Review the people you depend on for success at work, school, church, and personal hobbies. Assess these areas regularly to recalibrate when needed.

If you find your relationship to be in a state that you aren't comfortable with or didn't expect, take some time to evaluate the situation and your reaction to it. Make yourself get up earlier, stop at a park on the way home, stay up later to deal with the situation. This is how you empower yourself. You take 30 minutes out of the day to focus on yourself and that connection. Focus on the way you are reacting to your current life situation.

Maybe you'll find that you are where you want to be with no desired changes. I truly wish that for each of you. But I think more people will find that they're not entirely at peace with their current situation. These people will need to dig internally to find out what changes they should make. The next step is seeing if those changes are even feasible. Talk with the people involved and get their feedback. Then go through the process again. Evaluate your situation, develop a plan to change it, take action, and reevaluate your situation.

As we move through the scenes of my life, we can see a pathway emerging. This pathway is not straight and narrow. It is wide and turning, twisting back on itself even. Sometimes we have to experience things multiple times to learn the lesson or get the good from it.

Chapter 7
Our Daily Mask

"Behaviour is the mirror in which we can display our image." - Ghandi

Stonehenge Apartment

By 1990 our rent had doubled and we needed to move to a more affordable home. We ended up moving only two months after Brent's father died. We found an apartment on Stonehenge for $550 monthly rent. We lived there for several years, not moving again until August 1994. When we moved in, Tony was 17 months old, and Norah was 5 months old.

The apartment had much smaller closets, and it was on the second floor. There were only four apartments in the building, set slightly into the ground like a split level. The lower apartments had to go down about 4 or 5 steps to get to their units, while we had to go up about 8 steps to get to ours. The laundry was in the hall downstairs.

Both Tony and Norah were in diapers at

this time as they were not potty trained until about their third and second birthdays, respectively. I mostly used cloth diapers for them because of the lower cost than disposable diapers. I was home with them anyway. I tried couponing when we lived there. Since I wasn't working, I figured it was my contribution to the family.

Now looking back, my biggest contribution was being an at-home mom because that avoided the cost of daycare, work clothes, a car for work, lunches, etc. At the time, I didn't like it, though. I was 18 years old, and this was not necessarily the plan I had for this time in my life. Instead of moving into a new apartment, I should have been moving into a dorm room at SIU and entering my second year studying architecture.

I had had it all planned out. I was going to get my architecture degree and then intern at one of the big firms in Chicago. I'd get an apartment downtown and live the city life. I wouldn't need to own a car because everything would be within walking distance. I could visit the museums and neighborhood bars anytime. I would spend summer afternoons in the bleachers of

Wrigley Field with several friends - or make new ones there.

After about seven years of building my experience, I would branch out on my own. I would start "The Andersen Firm". The hallway into the company offices would be lined with three portraits - myself, my father, and my grandfather. I would eventually buy a penthouse apartment that had an incredible view of Lake Michigan and the city. I can still feel the excitement at the thought of building that life.

But I wasn't there. Life gave me another road to go on, and I wasn't afforded many opportunities to use my brain in the way I had been using it every day at school. My brain was just being used to look after and teach toddlers. I swear to you, I could feel my brain turning to mush daily. Toddlers will do that to you. I've learned that it doesn't matter if the mom is 18 or 38. Toddlers have this amazing power. However, toddlers also have the power to love and adore with complete abandon.

While living in the apartment on Stonehenge, we got married, had a third child, Jodi, bought our first cell phone, which cost about the same as one month's rent. I hated that Brent bought it because he knew I thought it was too expensive and unnecessary. He wanted to surprise me. He would use that tactic to justify his actions or to get something he really wanted. I disagreed with his assertion that we needed it. For a family of five who counted on the WIC (Women, Infant and Children) food program and family dinners to make it through each pay period, that was an obscene amount of money for something unnecessary.

We bought a new car while living there: a Pontiac 6000. A sedan with a sports engine. It was the showroom demo, and Brent was proud of that car. He used his inheritance from his dad to buy it.

I remember discussing with Brent if we were using the money for the right reason. Did it make sense to use this windfall for a car when we could use it as an investment in the future instead? We had that car for many years. I loved it and didn't want to get rid of it when we did, but we needed a bigger vehicle.

I didn't push the issue of using the money wisely for a few reasons. First, it was his inheritance from his father, not mine. We weren't married yet, so I didn't feel like it was ours together. Also, only being 18 myself, I wasn't confident about financial management.

I remember cracking the front bumper of that car on a tree during the winter one year. I was working at National Bank and Trust in the branch at Coltonville Road (also known as Rich Road). I loved working as a teller there. I hated having to leave, but I was so sick during my pregnancy with Jodi that I just couldn't stay.

I left work one winter evening and drove around the building to exit. The driveway around the side was curved in two places. One curve was nearly a 90-degree turn. I started sliding after the first curve and couldn't get control before it slid over the driveway's edge (there was no curb) and into the tree. I was hardly moving, so it only cracked the bumper, but, in true Brent fashion, he got very upset when I told him about it. He didn't ask how I was—maybe he assumed I was fine? Not sure. It would have been nice to have him ask.

While working for National Bank and Trust, I became pregnant with Jodi, our third child.

My third pregnancy was exceptionally difficult for some reason. With the first two babies, I was perfectly healthy. Maybe a bit too healthy with all the weight I gained each time. But, this time, I was nearly always nauseous and rarely felt good. In fact, it got so bad that Brent questioned if I was faking feeling ill. I don't know what purpose he thought my faking it would serve, but I suppose that's how he felt.

I loved my job as a bank teller. We worked the drive-up window for the branch. I had regular customers I waited on daily and yet was insulated from the public too. It was the perfect job for an introvert. It was low stress. Everything was done during the day, nothing to take home and worry about. It was a great job for a busy mom of two, going on three children.

The downside of the job was that one of my co-workers wore a strong perfume. I think the scent was Tabu. She was a great lady and I loved working with her. But she was constantly spraying perfume on herself because she would take smoke breaks. After each interval, she would respray it. That perfume made me feel so ill. I worked until I was about seven months along with this baby. With the first two, I had worked a regular shift at the shoe store within 12 hours or less of going into labor.

We also locked ourselves out of that apartment a couple of times. The one time that sticks in my head was on Easter Sunday of '92 or '93. We were hustling out for church as it was always a struggle to get us all out the door on time. When we got to the cars, Brent and I realized neither of us had keys. We couldn't go anywhere and couldn't get back inside. Somehow we called Chris, one of our best friends, and he rescued us. He drove over with a ladder. We knew the front window was unlocked, also the largest window. But, because we were on the second floor, we couldn't get to it. He brought a ladder and used that to get to the window, popped the screen off, and climbed through the window onto the sofa.

We had to warn him to be careful where he stepped as he climbed in the window. The Easter Bunny had arrived, but the kids had not been able to hunt for eggs in our haste to get to church. Eggs were on the couch and floor, and we didn't want him to crack any. They were just plastic eggs, but still.

One night, I folded clothes and went to the kids' room to hang them up and put them away. While in there, I could hear the kids ask Brent where Mommy was. He told them to go look for me. I heard them coming, so I just stood still where I was. In plain sight next to the closet. They came in, looked around, and left without seeing me. Grinning, I sat down on the floor so we would be at eye level with each other if they came in. They came in again, looked around, and left without seeing me. I started quietly laughing as I didn't want to give away my position, but it was so funny. They had literally looked right at me! It wasn't until the third time they came looking that they found me! We laughed about that for a long time.

They raised the rent in subsequent years to $580. Who knew we could afford that on Brent's computer salesman salary? We thought we could manage it and some months we did well, other months we mismanaged our money terribly. Unfortunately, the mismanagement of money was just one of the many cracks in our relationship.

The Parsonage

In August of 1994, we moved into the parsonage of Grace UMC in Maple Park. No, we were not suddenly ministers in the Methodist church. The appointed minister was not interested in moving into the parsonage. He was a professor at NIU in DeKalb and had no intention of moving into the little tiny town where he would now be shepherding half the citizens.

That was a boon for us. We were still in the 2-bedroom, 1-bathroom apartment on Stonehenge in Sycamore with three children under 5. Tony was of age to start kindergarten that fall, and the idea of sending him to the Kaneland school district was appealing. Kaneland was the largest school district in the state and had a much better reputation than the DeKalb school district where the apartment was located.

The rent was only about $100 more than our apartment and so much more space. The parsonage was a 3 bedroom, 1 bath ranch on the corner of Elm and Liberty. It had a full, finished basement, an attached 2-car garage, a fenced-in backyard, and a sun porch—so much extra space.

Two weeks before we got the news of approval to rent the parsonage, Tony came down with chickenpox. Smack in the middle of summer. He woke up one morning with small red spots spreading across his torso.

My mother quickly confirmed it was chickenpox and advised that we get Norah and Jodi exposed so all can have it and be done. Of course, I feared getting it myself since I had not had the disease. We also feared infecting unsuspecting people at a friend's wedding early in August. But, after explaining the situation to the bride, she told us to come on up. I'm sure it would have messed up their plans because Tony was the ring bearer, and I think Brent was in the wedding.

We went to the wedding and had a wonderful, fun weekend bar-hopping in Wisconsin and celebrating our friends' marriage. At this point, I was once again a stay-at-home mom, so I looked for any excuse to get dressed up. I was wearing dressy clothes, heels, and the whole nine yards. We walked around to so many bars on the night of the rehearsal. The next day I wore heels again for the wedding and the reception. We had a very fun time, but my back and legs were killing me. They were used to flats and running shoes, not pinchy, but super cute, heels.

On the Monday after the wedding, I invited Aunt Gloria to come over and help me pack. Or at least help me wrangle the kids so I could get some time to pack. We only had two weeks to move out and clean the apartment to turn back to the landlord. Not much time when you have small children. Little did I know that the time would be shortened even more because I had chickenpox.

As I stood in front of the hall closet debating where to start with the sorting, I rubbed my hand up my arm and noticed a bump on the back of it. I immediately showed it to Aunt Gloria, who confirmed chickenpox once again. I knew I was in a race against the disease at that point. I rushed to pack everything I possibly could in that house before I was too sick to help.

I packed that house up as much as possible in five days' time. When our friends and family arrived on Saturday morning, it was all pretty much packed, and I was delirious with illness.

To this day, I don't remember large chunks of that weekend of moving. I know we had several people with trucks and trailers helping. I remember being put to bed on a pallet of blankets and pillows laid on the dining room floor of the new house while my bed was being made up. We had a waterbed at the time so the bed had to be assembled, filled, and heated before I could get in. That was an all-day affair. I remember my mom filling the bathtub with warm water and oatmeal and making me get in. It felt so good though. I don't know why I resisted. That oatmeal is a wonder when it comes to relieving itching.

I know my mother-in-law set up my kitchen as a help. I do greatly appreciate her efforts in that. But it took me some time to find things and get them where I wanted them. In the end, it was truly by the efforts of family and friends that we were fully moved that weekend.

I asked my grandma to help clean out the apartment in order to get it in condition to return to the landlord. I knew she would do a great job, and she did. Spic and span it was. But, as corporate landlords do, they wanted to fine us for a soap ring in the tub, among other things. I knew my grandmother would not leave a soap ring in the tub. I refused to pay. We negotiated an agreement where we didn't pay but we also didn't get our security deposit back. That was highly disappointing but solidified my resolve to not rent from a corporate landlord again.

During our time living in the parsonage, many family milestones were met. Tony started kindergarten that fall and Norah the year after. I went to work shortly after Tony began school. We found a sitter, Angie, who did daycare in her home and was reasonably priced. She had a boy the same age as Jodi, which would give her someone to play with. Norah was the oldest by quite a bit, but I think that worked for Norah. She was kind of a helper to Angie.

I started working at Old Second National Bank in Maple Park. My first job was in the mortgage servicing department. My primary duty was to reconcile the private mortgage insurance payments on all loans that required this coverage. Each morning, when I would arrive, my desk was stacked high with binders full of reports printed overnight from the dot matrix printer. These reports listed the loans and the insurance payments. I would sort through all the reports and confirm the payments were made.

My desk was a 6-foot folding table with a folding chair. My office supplies consisted of a push-button desk phone, a couple of pens, highlighters, and a ruler to keep my lines straight when viewing the reports. It was a very tedious job, but it started me in the mortgage industry, a career that has served me very well.

I enjoyed the work I did there. I felt useful and productive for the first time in a while. Taking care of little children is not for the faint of heart or weak of mind, even if you are their mother. Or maybe, especially if you are their mother.

In some ways, it was a difficult choice to go to work and not be at home with the kids anymore. Brent and I had wanted to be the people who raised our kids. But I just wasn't happy being home all the time. Financially this seemed to be the right time since Tony would be in kindergarten, and we only needed care for Norah and Jodi. We certainly could use the boost the paychecks would provide.

We bought our first-ever brand-new furniture from a retail store when we lived in the parsonage. It was a set of bunk beds and 2 dressers that are still in the family. They were wooden bunk beds with slats to hold the mattresses. The dressers were relatively small, but the girls were about 5 and 3 when we bought them, so the size worked for their little clothes.

I have a picture of them proudly sitting in their beds after putting them up. They were so excited. Norah, with her little short haircut my mom had given her. The moment that changed the course of their relationship forever.

Norah had gone to stay with my parents for a day or two with her siblings. It could have been for many reasons, the most likely of which I just wanted a break for a night.

While there, Norah mentioned she wanted a haircut so my mom decided she should just go ahead and do that. It would save me from paying for a haircut or finding the time to take her to the stylist. The problem was that mom cut the hair quite short. Norah's hair was just below her ears when it was all said and done. To this day, as a 31-year-old mom of four, Norah is still very careful about who she lets cut her hair. She may even still harbor a little grudge against her well-meaning grandma.

In that same picture on the new bunk beds, Norah's little sister Jodi had a huge smile on her face because she was included with her sister. That was always her favorite. To be included with her sister.

Norah would sometimes take advantage of being the big sister. She would have Jodi ask for something that she wanted. I guess she thought we couldn't say no to the cuteness of the younger girl. One of my favorite memories is when we went to McDonald's for dinner one night. Jodi would have been about 3, making Norah about 5 or 6. Each of the kids had a happy meal. I'm pretty sure Norah had a cheeseburger. But she needed ketchup.

I'm sure we had some, but it most likely wasn't enough. Norah loved ketchup. She would dip anything and everything in ketchup. She dipped green beans and peaches because her Aunt Rosie bribed her with funny money. So, at McDonald's that night, she needed more ketchup but was too shy to go to the counter to get it from the server. She ended up taking Jodi with her. As we watched them, we realized that Jodi was the one who asked for and received the ketchup, immediately giving it to her sister. We still tease Norah with that story today. It will be interesting to see if her twins do similar actions.

We implemented a "snack administrator" program with the kids. We got tired of them asking all the time for snacks. So sometimes, the kids were the snack administrators, so they chose who got what and when. Usually, this was on a weekend day when we were home most of the day, but I think it was a great way to show them some independence as well as decision-making skills. We didn't do it for those reasons, but that was definitely a good byproduct. So many of our parenting decisions had unintended consequences that were usually positive for us.

We were so blessed that way. Although I remember when Tony was an infant, we discussed how we wanted our kids to behave in public. We were at a restaurant eating dinner. Tony was in his little kanga-rock-a-roo seat on the table. A little boy in the booth next to us kept popping up and interrupting us. He was trying to talk to us and would constantly be interrupting. As we worked our way through that dinner, we decided to have our children behave in public if not any other time. I'd say it worked out well.

We also expected them to care for one another and stand up for one another. There was no fighting with each other like I've heard about in so many families. Sure, they argued some, but it wasn't knock-down-drag-out fighting or nasty name-calling like I've heard of in so many families. Through the years, I realized how blessed we are with the children loving each other and caring for each other in such away.

Of course, their parents did plenty of fighting, so maybe that's why they didn't... I don't know.

Cracks in the Facade

While we lived in the parsonage, our two closest friends, Chris and Teddy, decided to get married—finally! They had been dating since high school, 5 years now. They had been so helpful and the most accepting of all our friends with the kids. They didn't leave us to our own devices or forget about us as their friends.

There was one moment when Teddy pulled me aside that was a bit difficult. We were hanging out at the house, kids playing outside, Brent and Chris shooting the breeze. Then, Teddy followed me out to the garage and said she wanted to talk to me about something. I could tell she was anxious regarding what she had to say but had no clue what it would be about.

I can still see the garage behind her: the plywood shelves along the side wall with various boxes and cartons piled to the ceiling. Many, if not all of the things in the boxes, are no longer with me today. The cars were not in the garage for some reason. They were on the driveway. Maybe the kids had been riding their bikes in the garage—if the weather was dicey we would do that sometimes.

She brought up the wedding and said she wanted to tell me something that Chris had said. They were talking about the wedding party and who would be their best man and maid of honor. I did not get my hopes up as Teddy had 3 sisters, so no shot. She said that Chris felt Brent was his best friend but was uncertain about asking him for that role. His reasoning was the strained relationship Brent and I had at times. Specifically, how Brent would treat me. He didn't want to say anything directly to Brent necessarily, but he wanted Brent to know that if he was going to be in the wedding, he would need to take steps towards improving our relationship.

Well, you could have knocked me over with a feather when she said this to me. I knew that sometimes he would say or do things I didn't like but I didn't realize how much it was obvious to and affecting others. Looking back now, it's a little embarrassing that I stayed in the marriage as long as I did. But I also knew at the time that I was doing what I thought was best. After all, marriage is to be until death. The problem is, what death? Not just the death of a spouse, but the death of love, honor, respect, even just simply caring for your spouse.

After that conversation, I thought long and hard about what she said. Was I being mistreated? Should I be demanding more respect from him? Was it worth the struggle, energy, tension?

Eventually, late one night, while lying in bed, I broached the subject with Brent. I told him straight up what Teddy said. "Chris doesn't want you for his best man unless you make some changes in how you treat me." Word for word, what she said. I don't remember a big blow-up or response. I remember that we talked it through, he wanted to know more about what things Chris was referring to. I don't remember him asking me how I felt about how I was treated, which now I think is interesting. That is typical narcissistic behavior, to think about what he has to do to get to the goal or reward. Not to think about how he deals with people in his way. Now I know that.

That conversation was the catalyst for going back to our marriage counselor. We had started seeing her when I was pregnant with Jodi. We went mostly because Brent was upset with me for always feeling sick and even thought I was faking it. Why I would do that with pregnancy number three and not with the first or second is anyone's guess.

For a counselor, we found an older lady in St. Charles and visited her several times to work out some differences. I think some issues were helped, but I think some were not. I also think that our time with her helped with our communication with each other, but I learned over the years that it never truly stuck. We'd be fine as long as we were in constant counseling. But, about a week or two later, maybe a month if we did really good work, we'd be right back where we started again.

Over the years we went to several different counselors to get us through difficult times. Looking back, it feels like those difficult times were always dictated by him. He decided that I needed to get help for something.

Usually, he would decide we needed to address our sex life, or, more accurately, I needed to deal with my issues about sex. I could never give him enough sex. I swear, even if we had sex daily it wasn't enough. Like seriously? How is that not enough? For me, sex isn't such an earthshattering moment. Don't get me wrong, sex, when done right, feels incredible. But, to do it right, one must be extremely vulnerable with one's partner. And that is the core of the problem.

But it is my past, my story. Those events and moments all come together to make me the person I am today. To make my children the people they are today. To make my ex the person he is today. I think we would all agree we are pretty good people today and in a good place mentally. My children all lead productive, happy lives and have healthy relationships with their chosen mates. Their children are happy, thriving children. I am blessed beyond measure.

On The Move...Again...

Through the years, Brent and I have tried many different options for additional income. One of those options was to become Amway distributors. During our tenure, we found ourselves making trips for conferences. We took our baby girl with us to Miami for a conference when she was only 2 weeks old. It was the first time I had been to Miami. Maybe Brent too, I honestly do not know. Miami is a fascinating city. South Beach architecture is famous for its Art Deco stylings. As someone who appreciated different architectural styles, the trip was a real treat for me.

Another one of the trips sent us to Atlanta in the spring of 1993 when they had a massive blizzard across the southeast. It made for quite a mess in the city with not enough equipment for clearing the snow. We stayed a day or two extra but then decided to trek home. It was quite a challenge to make our way through the icy and slippery interstates across the south, still covered in snow even days later. It took about 24 hours for us to get from Atlanta to Chicago. We ended up driving so far west, and when we realized we wouldn't outdrive the snow that way, we finally turned north.

A third trip was to Bristol, Tennessee. Bristol is a unique city because it sits on the border of Tennessee and Virginia. This is quite beautiful country. We spent time in the Cherokee National Forest. Climbed to the top of a hill that felt like we were climbing up a mountain. But it was so beautiful, I really didn't mind at all. We stood in that very park and determined that we needed to move our family south. We loved Bristol but knew it could prove foolish to narrow our options to such a small geographic area.

I feel that might have been one of the times we were truly in sync during our marriage when we were planning to move south.

We had a lot of conversations about where we would want to go. Of course, the first step was getting a job in an area we wanted to live in. Brent had been working in computer sales for a while by this time.

We started looking for jobs in the south, anywhere, really. We also looked at jobs in the north to eventually relocate to the south. So we had a combined purpose and goal. We found ourselves to be quite happy with how we worked together, each using our strengths to manage this process.

A few months later, Brent got a call from one of the online companies expanding into new markets and looking to hire sales and territory managers for these new markets. Eventually, he was offered the position, and he started working for them in their Chicagoland office.

After just a few months, he was offered a new market location, Minneapolis. Uh, no, thank you. Shortly after that, they offered Boston. I don't think so. We want to go south, but if not south, to somewhere we can comfortably raise our family. The third offer was much more aligned with our plans: Charlotte, North Carolina. Yes, indeed, yes! We were so excited about this prospect!

We immediately called our realtor to start working on the house sale. The kids were out of school for the summer, so we put them to work sorting their rooms, toys, etc. Getting rid of anything they felt they should get rid of. It's quite therapeutic to shed excess belongings.

By Labor Day 2000, the house was sold. Brent had been in North Carolina for a few weeks already and had found a house for us to rent. For the final three weeks in Illinois, the kids and I stayed in my grandparents' RV at my parents' house. School had not started in Illinois yet but had started in Charlotte a few weeks earlier, so we had some informal homeschooling.

My dad took on the science course by spending time with the kids outside teaching them to identify the kinds of trees, flowers, and plants. Mom had the kids help with harvesting from the garden. My aunt, an elementary school teacher, provided math worksheets for the kids to use.

It was a fun few weeks really. The kids were able to experience much of my childhood: playing with kittens, working in the vegetable garden, picking delicious fruits, and eating them while standing barefoot in the garden dirt and soaking in the warm sunshine. It's the most delightful way to eat fresh fruits and vegetables.

We packed up the rental truck on Labor Day weekend and put the van on the trailer behind it. We threw a large party with friends and family—so many people because we invited anyone we had known. We all hung out for the entire day together. Some people popped in and left again, but most people stayed for the entire time. I kissed all the babies, played with all the children, had my share of libations, and generally enjoyed the day.

The next morning came quickly as we were up before the sun to get on the road. Three kids and I drove in our green Olds 88 while Brent and one kid drove the truck. They were all to take turns going from the car to the truck. We had walkie-talkies to use to communicate with each other too. Before cell phones were in everyone's hands, this was a plan we came up with to make everyone happy.

The kids were so excited about our new adventure, but I think at this point, it was the road trip to a new place they were most excited about. There had been many tears shed over the last couple of days as we said our goodbyes to so many loved ones. Now it felt good to be happy, excited, and looking forward again.

We had estimated the drive to take about 12 hours. At some point, while driving in the mountains, we were detoured off the interstate onto tight, winding mountain roads with semi-trucks all around. It made me rather nervous but we had no plans to stop anywhere overnight so we had to charge on. After what seemed like hours and it felt like it was the middle of the night, we finally made it out to an interstate again. By now, I was just flat-out exhausted. We had been on the road for 18 hours straight. I radioed up to talk to Brent and tell him I needed a break.

We ended up pulling over on the side of the highway. The kids were all sleeping, Brent and I met at the back of the truck and I pro-

Chapter 8
Showing the Truth

"Sometimes it's not the people who change, it's the mask that falls off." - Haruki Murakami

People in your life will always treat you the way they feel about you. Someone who values your presence will treat you with kindness. Someone who doesn't see your worth will treat you with condescension. They may act impatiently. That does not mean they are correct. You are worthy of kindness, time, and attention.

If someone is treating you poorly, it is wise to evaluate that situation. First, determine if this is acceptable to you to be treated the way they do. If you want to be treated better, then fight for it. No one else will do it for you.

I don't remember the first time someone used the word "narcissist" to describe my husband. But it certainly was an accurate description. According to Psychology Today, the traits of narcissism include "a hunger for appreciation or admiration, a desire to be the center of attention, and an expectation of special treatment reflecting perceived higher status ." Manipulative behavior is also a trait of narcissism, according to WebMD.

I consistently saw these traits and behaviors from my husband, but I didn't put it all together until that word, narcissism, was used.

When Brent chose to ignore my concern about the purchase of a cell phone instead of focusing on our family's more immediate needs, the facade began to crack. His choice was made to reflect the "perceived higher status" that was always important to him. With each decision he made, my trust level dropped, and my awareness of his need to be right increased.

When we purchased the fancy car with his inheritance from his dad, it was again about perception. It was about showing off how well we were doing. We both had some insecurity about being teen parents and married so young. Unfortunately, those insecurities often lead us to make bad financial choices.

We had to rely on family during many of life's milestones for the funds to participate. Whether it was extra money for the security deposit on a new rental or fixing the car's transmission when traveling on a road trip we couldn't afford, we relied heavily on family to make our ends meet. To this day, not all the debts have been paid, and it's a source of embarrassment for me. The insecurities and misgivings I held deep inside of me rise as I remember the times we borrowed money over and over again.

With our young ages and Brent's propensity for acquiring speeding tickets, the last car we should have bought was a performance car. The insurance costs were astronomical, the payments were too high for us, but, this car fitted the right perception. I went along with it because I got excited about the idea of a brand new car. I let my excitement grow and pushed down the uncertainties. It was easier than fighting my husband.

The number of times I bit my tongue, chose not to argue, or just gave up on a disagreement because I knew it was going nowhere would probably rival the number of stars in the skies. As the years went on, these insinuations became his overt statements. Even though I knew many of his assertions of my character were not accurate, it was difficult to remember that when

I would hear them repeatedly.

Brent would find ways to show me how superior he was. For years I thought it was just his insecurities. I thought that deep down inside, we were alike. I thought he didn't believe he was valuable or worthy of good things or a good life. Or at least that he questioned that.

Often our arguments would include Brent telling me how much I was like my mother. This was said in a derogatory way. Through the years of hearing him say this over and over, I gradually let my relationship with my mom become tainted. I grew farther and farther away from my mom because it was easier than getting Brent to see her differently.

One of the many marriage counselors pointed out once that Brent saw my mom as a threat to his control over me. Wow, that's dark. But it also made sense.

I don't think my mom wanted to control me, but she probably could see Brent's actions differently than I could. As a mother, she could see how his behaviors and needs would affect me. She saw my personal transformation way before I knew about it. Much like mothers through the centuries, she knew me better than I knew myself at times.

When the counselor made that statement about the struggle for control of me, I was actually pissed for a long time at both Brent and my mom. How dare either one of them think that I was simple-minded enough to be controlled.

Eventually, I would reconcile my relationship with my mom, and I would understand she didn't want to control me. Her concern was directly a result of watching me change into a different person through my marriage. She didn't engage with Brent to fight for control of me but rather to fight for me to have control over myself.

Chapter 9

Passive Turns Aggressive

"Only a man who doesn't love himself,
mistreats the woman who loves him."
- r.h. sin

Housekeeping

I've never been one with a worry about housekeeping. I received a poem from someone when Tony was born that said:

"Cleaning and scrubbing can wait til tomorrow for babies grow up, we've learned to our sorrow. So quiet down cobwebs, dust go to sleep. I'm rocking my baby and babies don't keep."

That poem has been my life's mantra, especially when choosing between family time or cleaning. I like to think I'm better at keeping house than my mom, but then she never boasted at her own prowess regarding those abilities anyway. But my kids are definitely better than I was at housekeeping.

During a recent visit to my daughter Jodi,

she told me that she and Norah would like me to do the Marie Kondo thing at my place. They want me to hold each possession I have and determine if it "sparks joy". If it does, I can keep it. If it doesn't, I would need to get rid of it.

I think I do pretty good with sorting and purging, but she says it's the clutter. Well, yes, I will concede clutter has been an issue for me.

The irony is that I was thinking about how my kids are much better at keeping house than I was, and I'm so glad for them. I like a nice neat home, but I can't seem to keep it that way. So this afternoon I sent a text to Norah and told her that if she truly wanted to help me with this, I'd be more than happy to accept it. No answer yet, but in fairness, I think she's at work.

Brent was never fastidious about housekeeping either. I'm pretty sure he always viewed that as my job. In the same way that he viewed the cooking, the bulk of the children's discipline and decisions were my responsibility. Yet he would feel compelled to put in his two cents even when I wasn't asking for it. I also knew that if I didn't follow his recommendation, he would be sure to remind me if my plan failed and gloat if his plan was successful. He would often make fun of how my mother kept the house. Again attempting to manipulate my relationship with her. While I understand why he made comments about her housekeeping, making fun of someone, especially if someone is your wife's mom, isn't the most flattering of actions.

If someone were coming to visit, then he'd be on the ball about cleaning. So much so that it would drive me nuts. Super intense. And things had to be perfect when we had a visitor. It was quite exhausting to keep the house clean, work full time and put up a façade of the "perfect family". It takes so much more energy to perpetuate a lie than to allow the truth to be revealed.

He would make comments like, "We live in a shithole." His passive-aggressive way of telling me I wasn't keeping up with the house, laundry, etc. After years of this, I finally decided to let the outdoor chores go. I love to garden—vegetables and flowers. But something had to give as I realized I couldn't do it all. Then he started griping because I never helped him in the yard.

After 15 years of trying to keep up, actually 16 if you count the time we lived together before marrying, I just knew it wasn't going to happen. So I started ignoring his comments about my lack of help with the outdoor chores. Never mind that I was the only one cooking dinner each night. Never mind that I was the only one focusing on laundry even though I had asked repeatedly for assistance with it. Sure he would help for a few days at most and then fall off again. His job was always okay for him to spend a million hours a week on, but not me.

It was a mirror for how lopsided our relationship was. I did the work, and he would come in and collect the reward, soak up the praise, enjoy the moment. He may say the same thing about me because from his perspective, it may have felt that way. He would maybe fill in different things—like he would be the one to say he did all the yard work and grilling out while I sat in the house watching TV or playing with the kids or doing crafts. Certainly, he would not indicate I was working hard. But this book is about my perspective, not his.

Leading The Way To Uncertainty

He would say he took the lead in our relationship too. He would mean that he took the lead in our physical relationship. After a time, I just gave up and let him do as he wished. I was not excited about sex with him and did not want it. But, as a wife, there are certain duties you perform, right? At least, that's what I told myself. Our counselor called it "mercy fucking." I completely related to that term. That's exactly what I was doing, but he continued to demand more physical intimacy even after the counselor identified it and understood what that meant. The problem is, that's like demanding respect, it's just not how that works.

Physical intimacy requires trust. I'm not sure I ever trusted my husband beyond the first few years. But that trust was fully destroyed when, on Easter morning of 2008, he revealed to me that he had cheated on me. He told me about a time at a work conference with the office admin and other co-workers. His story went like this:

One night they all were at the bar, he was drinking too much, and she was too. He was concerned about her and helped her to her room. Of course, he stayed in the room with her as she went to the washroom to make sure she would be safe and tucked into bed after. But, the temptation of knowing she was naked in the washroom was too much from him to not act. He says there was never actual intercourse, but I don't know that it matters. The fact he would go that far was too much for me.

My reaction to his confession was a complete and total shock that quickly dissolved into total grief. I couldn't understand it at all. Why would he jeopardize our life this way? For a little quickie? It made me wonder if he really did only that. He never admitted to more but the damage to the relationship was done.

I always felt that he was too dominating in bed and other aspects of our relationship. That's one reason I did not like sex necessarily. It was his way or the highway, just like the rest of our marriage. That's probably the worst thing you can do to a sexual molestation survivor: not let them have control of their own body.

Since my marriage ended and I dated other men, had relationships with other men, and subsequently married my amazing husband, I have come to find out its not sex that I don't like. Instead, it's the emotional factors that accompanied sex in my first marriage that I didn't like.

Looking back at this time, I can see his confession was the true beginning of the end of our marriage. Don't get me wrong, I fought like hell to keep it together. I journaled, prayed, meditated. I suggested dates and tried to spend time with him doing things he enjoyed. We went to a counselor again. This time we went to a man as I thought maybe he could relate better to Brent and really help us dig into the trust issues.

A couple of years later, I took a personal retreat to evaluate my thoughts on the marriage. During that retreat, I rededicated myself to keeping the marriage together. I read books on how to reinforce your marriage after infidelity. I talked with Brent about these ideas and techniques. But a marriage cannot be saved by one person alone. It takes two to make it work. Brent had started to mentally check out of the relationship by this time.

I look at my journals from this time, and

there are budgets based on my income to see if I could afford to live separately. There are calculations for child support. Listing of debts and assets and how they could be split. It wasn't until I read through my journals for the project of this book that I realized I did these things at this time. I thought it was much later that I seriously thought of divorce. I realize now that I was starting to value myself in a way that my husband never would.

Maybe all the prayer, journaling, and meditating brought this to me, but I know I was looking at myself as a stronger person than before the infidelity happened. I knew what it was now to be confronted by such a horrible abuse of trust and survive it. The saying "what doesn't kill you makes you stronger" is very true. By becoming stronger, I learned to be more proactive in asserting my needs, not just trying to meet everyone else's. I started doing things on my own instead of frustrating myself by begging Brent to come along. I started reading again no matter what comments I might receive. Taking back that little bit of control was vital to me becoming the person I am today.

The Grand Palm

The summer of 2010 was a tough one. Not knowing where my children would sleep in the near future drove anxiety sky high. The unsettled feelings of how I would provide shelter for them dominated my days and tormented my nights. A constant feeling of unease and uncertainty followed me through all my waking hours.

After a rocky spring of losing a job, getting a job, losing a job, finally admitting the need to file bankruptcy, losing a car to repossession, filing the bankruptcy and all the while knowing we could not afford to live in our home anymore, I was exhausted emotionally.

For the past few weeks, I had worked from home for a mortgage loan processing company as a contract processor. The problem was that there was not enough work to keep me busy or to pay the bills. I'd been working in the upstairs office with the windows open to avoid turning on the AC. Everything was covered with pollen daily, and I found myself cleaning the space each morning. But, by noon, my hands had that rough feeling that announced I was covered in pollen once again. I was sure this was not good for my computer and printer. And the humidity in Georgia didn't help either.

But, there I sat, looking out the window at my kids playing basketball on the driveway, wondering where we would live when the bank foreclosed. Would we even be able to rent a place large enough for two adults, four nearly grown children, and two dogs? How much was that going to cost? How much for a pet deposit? The only reason we got the dogs six years earlier was that we bought the house. But now we would lose it. It was just a matter of time.

We always seemed to have rough times financially. Even when we both made more money in one year than ever before, we still struggled. Finances were just another subject in our relationship that we could never get in sync.

My parents had taught me to save money. Whenever I received pay from a babysitting job or detasseling corn, I put half the money into savings and I could use the other half anyway I liked. I remember putting more than half into savings because I didn't really need to spend money for anything.

My parents would demonstrate their bill-paying for the whole family. They would collect the bills and checkbook in the top left drawer of the green desk that sat in our kitchen. Each week, they would pull that drawer out of the desk and set it on the table, setting out the bills, checkbook, and calculator. My mom or my dad would then sit down and sort out how much money was in the checkbook and how much the bills were for that week.

My siblings and I knew when the green desk was missing a drawer, it was bill paying time, and therefore steer clear of the kitchen if you could. It wasn't that my parents were mean. It just was one of the few times when our home had high tension. So it was better to steer clear if possible.

The home I created with Brent was quite the opposite in many ways, but most certainly regarding finances. We had a lot of tension in our home all the time because of our difficult relationship. But, the tension was significantly higher when it came to money matters.

Brent was not taught about money management at all by his parents. From what I could discern, his father did pretty well caring for his funds. I truly do not know about his mother during his younger years. As she has gotten older, I know that she has done well with managing her funds.

When Brent was a teenager, he was not required to save any of his paycheck so he did not. Instead, he spent each dollar each week and some weeks, spent more. Then he would have to sweet talk his mother into a bit of a loan. I remember seeing the ledger of how much he owed his mother from these little loans. It was quite a bit in my estimation. But, as a teenager, I didn't realize how important this information should have been in determining the future of my relationship with Brent.

Between the instability of our financial situation through the years and my current employment situation, which found me making far less than I was capable of, it created a deficit we would not be able to overcome. Previously, with our financial uncertainty, I had not had to worry that my children would have no place to lay their heads at night. Now I was not even thinking about safety or comfort. Just a basic roof over their heads.

Some would say fix up your house and sell it as a quick solution. But, at this particular time in history, the real estate bubble had burst. The market was so bad, and we had leveraged all we could in the preceding years to make improvements. We were now upside down by quite a bit. We owed more on the house than we could possibly hope to gain by selling.

We requested a modification based on my income drop and job losses I had suffered since I was still working in mortgages. This process was started months earlier, but it was still in process. In the end, no one knew if or when we would get any relief from that request.

I shuddered to think what my credit score must have looked like. It was surely at the bottom of the barrel. This would add to the difficulty in getting a rental home as most landlords want good credit—understandably so. Which meant an apartment was the next best option, and I hated having corporate landlords. Every time I had a corporate landlord, they charged me stupid amounts for made-up repairs and cleaning after I moved out. It's a racket.

This brought me back to the main issue, the reason for my many sleepless nights and untold anxiety.

The modification package was returned for more documentation. I'm not sure why they kept sending the entire package back. How obnoxious! Each time we had to start over at the end of the line.

Collecting paperwork to document our loss of income over the last couple of years and crafting letters of explanation about these circumstances were the reason for my existence in those days. It was probably a good thing I didn't have any loans to process since I doubted I could focus on them anyway.

W2 forms, tax return documents, employment verifications, letters explaining employment dates, salary amounts, benefits allowed and accepted were stuffed in this envelope. Yet somehow, it was still not enough information to determine that we couldn't make our payment. I guess I needed to make a late payment for them to realize we were seriously in trouble here. Although, I would have thought that the bankruptcy and car repossession would be clues enough. Maybe they thought we could make the payments easily now because we didn't have those payments? I didn't know what else they could be thinking.

I had been out of work for some time at that point. And that was after months, if not years, of being paid less than I had previously been making. After several months, we finally got the modification, although it didn't change the payment nearly as much as we had hoped.

Teenagers

Many years after becoming a mom, I finally realized its true gift. That summer, the one so filled with anxiety, worry, and concern, gave me time to bond with my kids and learn who they were in a way I never realized was so vitally important.

Not to say I didn't have "mom feelings" many times throughout my life, but it wasn't until this summer, when I was home with my all teenage crew, that I realized just how beautiful, extraordinary, and unique they each were. I learned that summer just how vital my kids were to my happiness. Even in the midst of the anxiety and worry about the house and the finances, this was probably some of the best bonding times I'd had with my kids. I think these may have been the times when I stumbled upon developing the relationships that I now enjoy tremendously with my kids. They all are unique, loving individuals who make such an impact in their circles of influence.

I'm incredibly proud of how they all turned out, and I truly believe it has to do with being authentic, admitting my mistakes to them when needed, but also giving their lives to God as often as I could remember to do so. I still pray for them and their families (future and present) and will do so for the rest of my life. I may not remember all the birthdays for all the grandchildren, nieces and nephews like my grandmother did until her dying day, but I will remember the love, the joy, and the beauty of life with them.

Peter the Entrepreneur

Our fourth child, Peter, has always had the heart of an entrepreneur and made that clearly known before middle school. He tried multiple times with friends to start a lawn-mowing business. Unfortunately, they never really got off the ground. But he kept trying and had some success with other ventures.

When Peter was in middle school, I noticed that we were going through a lot of gum as a family. I found this to be strange since at least 2 of my kids wore braces at the time, and I was pretty particular about them not chewing gum. Let's be honest, though. I'm sure they did some. That said, I still had a big gum shortage happening and didn't know why. Then, one night at dinner, one of the kids commented to Peter about his business and how it was going. He tried to hush up the conversation, which was all the more reason why I would not let the conversation end.

Asking the other kids to explain further what they were talking about, I discovered that Peter had been selling gum on the bus. Gum that he was taking from our kitchen drawer.

That was apparently the source of the gum shortage. We had a conversation about paying supplies that night.

Peter has gone on to become quite the entrepreneur. He recently sold his first business and is starting up a second one. That business was built while working full time as a restaurant manager and a realtor.

Can You See It?

Shortly after one of my parents' visits, when my mom and I had talked about my concerns over my relationship with Brent, she suggested that I not engage with him when he was being unreasonable or difficult. I remember feeling like that was such a great idea and wondering how I hadn't thought of it before! I committed myself to using this approach, especially when others were around, to lessen our friction and hopefully improve our times together.

There were times when I would think Brent was just picking at me for no reason. Actually, it felt like most times. But, I was thinking, if only one of his relatives—his brother or sister-in-law or cousin—could see this behavior, maybe they could explain it to him in a way that would get him to stop.

Once when JuJu was visiting, I felt that Brent was constantly picking at me. I remember standing in my kitchen making dinner with JuJu while chatting. It was a gorgeous sunshiny Georgia day. Brent was outside on the deck. As he came through the kitchen, he made a snarky comment to me. I forget now what he said, but I know that I had said nothing to him on this occasion.

I followed my mother's advice and did not even reply when he did that. Reacting to him never produced anything good, it would always just spiral downward. As he left the kitchen, I let out a breath I didn't even realize I'd been holding.

I looked at his cousin and asked, "Was that me? Did I say something to him to deserve that?" She, who never inserts herself into family squabbles, said, "I understand what you mean now." That validated me.

At this point, my emotions were on their last breath. I was really just looking to confirm I wasn't crazy for thinking I hadn't done anything to deserve the snarkiness. Prior incidents had left me feeling inferior in some way, stupid or irrational. Just trying to defuse the situation even though I didn't know what the situation was. This kind of abuse had been happening for years and, as far as I could see, would continue to happen until and unless I separated myself from the situation.

Chapter 10
Trust In The Timing

"It is never too late to be who you might have been." - George Eliot

Trusting God

God's timing is always the best. Even though many times it feels like He's not paying any attention to your life and needs, He does have your best life in His hands. I look back at the anxiety-ridden summer of 2010 and realize that even though it was heavy with worry and anxiety, I learned that summer to give my fears and cares over to God continually.

I do not always hand everything over to Him as I should. But that was the summer I learned how much that works and if you can do it, it changes your life if you allow it to. The key: it must be a choice to turn over your worries to God. Choose to hand over your concerns because, quite honestly, God's got a plan for you, and if you get out of His way, it will all work out in the end. No endless amount of worry will alter His plans, but by acting outside of His best for you and acting before it is the right time, you can change your life.

What's your biggest issue right now? That one thing that just popped in your head as you are reading this book. What is it? Name it. Journal about it, pray over it, ask God for His guidance, and then GIVE IT TO HIM.

In the past, I have made the motion of handing over my worries to God many times. I physically moved my hands upward and outward while opening my tightly clenched fists to a flat palm. We would take this action to hand an item over to another person. Using this action, this physical movement, to truly give it over to Him helps release the worry.

God has everything worked out, and in the end, you'll feel silly for all the time, energy, and embarrassing actions you took while stressing yourself out over the issue. It's just that simple. Yet so very, very difficult.

Becoming Stronger

Learning to stand up for yourself is a terrifying proposition when you've spent years and years being pushed down. Especially when you still have not realized that you have been pushed down and made to feel inferior. How can you see your value when you see yourself through the eyes of someone who constantly finds fault with what you do and how you do it?

Motherhood has a way of making us doubt ourselves and our abilities. Nothing in life challenges us as a child does with their own ways and ideas. As a young mother, I struggled with my identity and valuing what I gave to my children. What could I, as a teenage mom, a screw-up, a failure, have to offer these kids other than getting them through each day safely, fed, and with shelter? My self-worth dropped to an all-time low during these early years of motherhood.

As my life went, these years also coincided with the early years of my marriage. Did this lack of self-worth influence my marriage? Surely it did. Brent thought he was getting a fun-loving, vivacious teen girl as his bride when inside, I was a scared little child with no confidence and even less self-worth. That is not a good way to start any relationship, and least of all, one of the most important relationships of your life.

Through the years, I gained confidence when I would excel at work or in my home duties somehow. For example, cooking was a great source of pride. I fed my family well—sometimes I made mistakes—but overall, they were well fed. I'm a good cook. After over 20 years of cooking for a crew of six, I know this now. But now, in my empty-nester life, cooking is not a vital skill in the same way it was when the kids were all at home.

When I say I'm a good cook, there was still one very notable incident. Brent always hated soup, but I loved making it. I loved experimenting with recipes.

One evening, Brent was gone overnight on a work trip, so I decided to try a new recipe - Cream of Broccoli soup. I know that may sound strange, but my kids and I all loved broccoli so we were excited about this new recipe. I cooked and measured, blended and cooked and measured some more. Finally, I dished up five bowls, one for each child and myself. We all sat down to the table in anticipation of what surely would be our new favorite.

Upon viewing the bowl of what appeared to be green mushy grits and smelling the pungent aroma, I knew it was all a waste. There was no way even I could eat this. It was so unappealing.

Quickly scooping up each bowl before the children could even assess the contents, I declared we would order pizza instead. This was the most humiliating cooking attempt in my life.

But despite those minor missteps, I kept striving for the confidence to live my life in a way that would please God. He is the source of confidence, and His presence makes our life on earth worthwhile. I learned that God needed to be the center. If we can help each other on this earth, we can be assured of doing His work.

Gaining confidence in myself was mainly developed by studying the Bible, journaling, and surrounding myself with women who had gone through similar trials to those I experienced.

God put the right people in my path, even when I didn't know they were the right people. For example, I had a great boss with whom I'm still friends today. He helped me see the value of myself simply by trusting me to do my job and run the office when he was not there. That relationship taught me that we all—bankers, CEOs, janitors, and loan processors—put our pants on one leg at a time. No one is greater than or lesser than anyone else.

As Eleanor Roosevelt once said, "No one can make you feel inferior without your consent." Choose to live your life as a worthy, valuable person. Don't act superior to others, but don't let yourself feel inferior either.

Chapter 11
Knocked Sideways

"Being ignorant is not so much a shame, as being unwilling to learn." - Benjamin Franklin

I am gay.

Those three little words rocked my world. They came from my then-15-year-old cousin, a sweet teenager I had known from before she was born. All I could feel was a sadness for her. But why? I thought her life was going to be rife with struggle and fear. I wanted to protect her from people who would harm or judge her. I never once questioned my love for her. That was inconceivable to me and I completely supported her.

I am a Christian, was then and still am. However, as we all know, some teachings in the Bible arguably state that homosexual relations are "abominable" to God. I am not going to get into a debate about gay lifestyle, but having this dear child say this to me made me think twice.

I know this child. Like I KNOW her. I was

there at her birth, watching as her mother labored and worked and pushed to bring her forth in this world. I cared for her as an infant. Then, as she grew, I watched her learn to explore, be curious, ask questions. As she became a young woman, I watched as she learned to listen to her body and to believe in her own convictions, to be strong in ways that weren't physical. Yet, she figured out the physical too. Such a strong, beautiful, intelligent, seeking, questioning, loving, compassionate young woman.

I remember when she was in first grade and played basketball at our church. She had only been in the area for about 4 months and had not yet made many new friends, or so she thought.

Yet, when it came to the end-of-year awards ceremony, she won the most significant award. The one where all the coaches and facilitators came together and chose one boy and one girl out of all the first-to-fifth graders. The Christlike award. This award went to the child who showed the most characteristics of Christ: love, compassion, empathy, etc.

They announced the boy first. His family

stood beaming, so happy for him. The audience applauded and cheered. Then my sweet cousin was announced. The audience stood and hooted and hollered. They cheered like crazy! They started chanting her name over and over! It was the wildest thing!

When she was born, I knew that looking down into her beautiful baby face she was destined for greatness far beyond anything I could imagine. In my humanity, I thought maybe she'd be the President of the United States or another high-level politician and make real, lasting, effective change in the world. Maybe she'd be a missionary and go to places we'd never even heard of before. Maybe she'd do something that I couldn't even fathom because I am merely human. I felt this in my soul, heart, and mind. I still feel this.

Still, knowing all this, I find my mind swirling with questions and emotions at her announcement. I know this child. I know her heart. She has a heart for God. She is more connected to God than anyone else I know.

Why would God allow this to happen if it is so abominable to Him? He doesn't enjoy our suffering. His heart breaks when ours do. Yet, this was happening. It was really truly happening.

I had suspected this for a while. The clothes she was wearing, the friends she had or didn't, her lack of interest in boys as a 15-year-old girl. I remember talking to her mother about 4 months before her announcement about her clothing choices.

Not that I was going to make her wear something different, but so that she understood what the plaid button-ups with jeans and minimal jewelry and boots were saying to the world. And, again, not to create a peer pressure situation, but to prepare her for people's remarks. She was choosing plaid flannel shirts, jeans, ball caps, things one would look on as stereotypical lesbian clothing choices.

After her revelation, my sweet niece seemed to be lighter and happier than she had been in months. Her mother told us that she ended up spending more time with the family than she had in months after sharing her announcement. She had been feeling immense pressure about telling her family. If it means more family time, then this is all worth it. The next morning, my first thought upon waking was, "The world did not end and God is still on His throne!"

For the next 5 years, I wrestled with this announcement. How could my God, a God of love, allow His child to be gay—something He hates? This didn't make sense when I rationalized it with who I know this child to be and who I know my God to be. So for 5 years, I studied, researched, and explored the possibilities of what this lifestyle really meant to God and the world. I needed to know how she would be accepted in this world and what pitfalls to help her watch out for. Help her learn how to protect herself in this subsector of society that I knew nothing at all about.

My views on homosexuality were challenged, not just my faith. I thought it was an abomination too because that's what I thought God's message had been. I was challenged with accepting the sinner, but not the sin, loving the sinner and hating the sin.

I thought at first, maybe that's the lesson in it for me. So I worked hard to accept everything my cousin was telling me. I asked questions when I had them; I encouraged her to focus on her schoolwork and other activities first, and not to concern herself with relationships for now. It's too distracting when your goals are so huge to be in a relationship, and all the energy it takes to be emotionally invested with someone will take away from the energy you need for your goals.

As I worked through all of the emotions and challenges I felt during those 5 years, one of the thoughts I had about how to get to the bottom of the question of whether or not it is sin to act as a homosexual was to study Greek and Hebrew. If I studied those languages, I could then read the Bible in its original writings and determine for myself if God really said what is attributed to Him. While trying to find places to learn this and study the Bible in its original form, I continued to study, read, and pray.

I finally came to the conclusion that people are born as homosexuals. It was the only way it made sense to me at that time. I struggled with the modern interpretations of the Bible that said God abhors homosexuality. My cousin loves God and would not purposely sin against Him in such an obvious way. Therefore, since this is not a choice, it must be simply the way she was made. Why else would this girl choose a sinful, hard, and painful life? And, if it is a choice, why would God make someone that way, knowing those desires and feelings would lead to sin in His eyes?

During the 5 years I wrestled with this proclamation, I concluded that God is always loving, always knowing, and truly does work all things together for good. I also confirmed that the world would do what it is going to do and say no matter the Lord's counsel on any given subject. The world is going to see things without the lens of the Lord. I also understood that some people who profess to be Christians think it's best to push their agenda just as hard as the LGBTQ+ community pushes theirs. It makes me think about the theme of the Old Testament, which is an eye for an eye.

As time went on, my cousin continued to mature and explore the world around her. She graduated from high school and went away to college. During that time, her parents divorced. She tested relationships of her own. Eventually, she came to date a young man she had met and the two fell quickly and completely in love.

After talking with her about this man, I knew that she was indeed in love without a shadow of a doubt. Today, she is married to this young man and so very happy in her life as a mom. She is doing the "work" she is currently destined to be doing. And, someday, when the kids are all grown and life changes again, she'll still have that loving, compassionate nature, she is so well-known for and can choose to further her impact at that time.

Elliott's Journey

I first met my step-son Elliott in the fall of 2016. Assigned female at birth, Elliott was still going by Kristen and still presented as female when I first met him. I dated Elliott's dad Craig for a few months when I met Craig's two youngest kids. He spent every other weekend with them when they both would come to visit. His youngest would visit each time, but his son Elliott didn't always come.

When I met Elliott the first time, I already knew there had been a conversation about his need to be a man. Conversations about the urges to be male, about the feelings dating back to childhood—feelings of discomfort when wearing a dress or other feminine clothing.

When Elliott was a pre-teen, his parents divorced. This was a challenging time for him with all the changes a divorce brings. On top of this strain was all the uncertainty and angst of being a teen, going to a new school, and navigating changed family relationships. Additionally, while still presenting as a female, he had been attacked by someone he trusted. We feared that he was allowing his swirling emotions from all of these changes and situations to be the catalyst for transition.

After getting to know each other better over time, I better understood what it meant to transition. Elliott started to dress more gender-neutral and even a bit masculine when he was with us for the weekend. He felt comfortable doing so, and it made me happy to see.

There was still so much to learn. Elliott found out about a workshop for parents to understand what was happening with their child and asked us to go with him. Even though neither his dad nor I truly understood or could even wrap our minds around what it meant to have the feelings Elliott had been experiencing for years, we wanted to support him. We knew Elliott was unhappy, so attending the workshop was an easy way to support him. We did learn quite a bit during that evening and not even so much from the workshop facilitator. It was difficult to see all the pain and hurt that so many of these people were experiencing for simply wanting to be their true, authentic selves.

Elliott's dad and I had many conversations about transgender people and what that meant to us. There were also opportunities for me to talk with Elliott individually. These conversations were very helpful for me to understand better what all of this meant.

I needed time to process and learn, as did his dad. One of the biggest reasons for Elliott's unhappiness was because he had already, in his mind, identified as male, but we couldn't process this fast enough for him. The root cause of the unhappiness was simply that this young person could not fully embrace life as a male because the world didn't fully embrace him as a male.

While his dad and I encouraged Elliott to follow his path in life, we were also concerned about what that would mean. No parent wants their child to live life harder than necessary. That was the fear his dad and I felt for him. Living life presenting as a male was bound to lead to complex, heart-breaking situations.

Before Elliott graduated from high school, he and his brother Thomas came to live with their dad and me. This was a quickly developing situation. One week Craig and I were empty nesters. The next week, we had two teens to raise. Talk about major life changes!

Luckily, we were able to accommodate both of the kids and helped them settle in quickly. They moved in right at the end of the school year so they had all summer to get used to their new neighborhood. Neither of the kids had been involved in extracurricular activities or had jobs before. They had some chores to do around the house with their mom, but not a lot beyond school and friends.

One of the first things we encouraged the kids to do was find jobs. Elliott and Thomas had to be encouraged daily to job hunt, largely because they didn't know how to do it. We talked about how to present yourself in a business and walk in and ask for the manager to ask about job openings. We talked about what information would be needed on the applications and how to be prepared. As a result, they both submitted applications to numerous businesses and eventually were hired at different fast food restaurant locations.

They started working within just a week or so of each other. Thomas's experience was very positive. He enjoyed working, doing something with a sense of pride, and getting the payment reward. He enjoyed the social aspect of working too. He came home after each shift with a new friend's phone number. Usually, these were from girls his age, but he also made male friends and even some advantageous business connections.

Elliott's experience was not as good. The store manager was difficult to please and wasn't very good at communicating in a way Elliott understood. After a few months of this unpleasant experience, Elliott requested to be moved to Thomas's store.

His dad and I were not so sure that was a good idea. As much as Elliott and Thomas loved each other, they were siblings and tended to fight. We were concerned their sibling arguments would spill over into the workspace. We finally agreed to allow it as long as Elliott understood that Thomas was there first, so Elliott would have to transfer out or find a new job if it went sour.

When Elliott started working at the new restaurant with his brother, he requested a name tag with "Elliott." Unfortunately, this caused some confusion with his manager and co-workers because he had to complete all the paperwork with his dead name, Kristen, so they were thrown off from the start. Elliott felt discriminated against for this and for not being allowed to choose male uniforms.

This job went a little better than the first one because the restaurant was better managed. However, there were still some difficulties when it came to communication. These issues might have been less about gender expression than they were about not understanding or properly performing the job's duties.

Elliott continued to explore and experiment with what life presented as a boy would be like. His clothing choices were more masculine. Discussions about choosing a male name were brought up with his dad and me, much like a pregnant woman would do for her unborn child.

We struggled with these changes, including the request to call him Elliott and use male pronouns. His dad was not as concerned about the outer image as he was about the root cause for these requests and changes. It was easier for me to work with the changes Elliott wanted to make because I had only known him for a very short time before his transition. I tried to help bridge the gap between Craig and Elliott to keep communication open between them. I would explain how I felt when my cousin came out and what I had done to cope with the situation.

Elliott kept at it and insisted that life as a boy is what he was meant for instead of a female. Over time and through multiple requests, Craig eventually acquiesced and started to call Elliott by his new name. The first time that happened,

I was so excited and happy for all the family. As the dad, Craig's leadership in accepting Elliott was important for Elliott and the siblings. Even though Elliott's siblings wanted him to be happy, processing and accepting this was hard. It was great that Craig was accepting Elliott's being transgender.

Today Elliott is happily married to a woman who has supported him through all of the difficulties of coming out and starting the transition process—and it is a complex, expensive, emotional process. However, they are building a life for themselves and family relationships continue to grow in a positive direction.

Chapter 12
Becoming Kinder
"The best project you will ever work on is you!"
- Jennifer

The "so that" verse, 2 Corinthians 1: 3-4, tells us that God provides comfort to us and that we are to use that comfort to care for others. In verse 6, Paul tells us that if we are distressed or suffering, it is to help those we interact with. If we are helped, then so are those around us. We receive the patience to endure the same sufferings with each other. Creating a world full of hope and kindness should be our daily mission.

A colleague of mine once said her goal was to improve herself by 1% each day. Some days that means drinking 1% more water than she did the day before. Or maybe working out 1% longer or journaling 1% more in her diaries. The point is that if we each can just do 1% better each day, eventually, we can all become better together.

Kindness, just like meanness, has a ripple effect like water moving when something touches it. No matter if you throw a huge rock with a large plop or a butterfly flits to the surface of a still pond, the effect will continue outward toward the edges of the pond. But the choice is ours as to how we affect that pond.

Do we bulldoze through, cutting down anything in our path—the weeds and the flowers? Or, do we carefully make a path, loving the weeds and the flowers? At one time, all flowers were considered weeds anyway. So, maybe that person who just treated you abysmally is simply a weed needing some kindness, patience, and love.

Oh, how I remember the heartbreak when my cousin came out to me. I believed she would be living a life that would send her to hell. In desperation, I thought, How does she know this at 15? A friend countered that question with, "Didn't you know if you liked boys or not at 15?" I thought back to my teen years and agreed, yes, I did indeed know I liked boys. That question helped me make sense of the situation enough to think clearer.

Much like Elliott's situation, my cousin's family had just been through great emotional turmoil, and her daily life had changed drastically. I was concerned that she was going through a phase, looking for a way out of her complicated situation. My theory was that gay or transgender people simply don't like or understand themselves. They're not equipped to figure it out, or maybe it's too difficult. So it seems easier for the young adult to say I'm someone else.

Most people come out as gay or transgender as teens or even younger. These are times when their physical bodies are still growing, but even more importantly, their brains are still developing. When their hearts and souls are not yet mature, it's tough to figure yourself out, especially as a teen when things change moment by moment and "the rest of your life" seems like an unimaginably long time. But altering yourself chemically with hormone blockers and other pills seems like a huge risk. How do you know that in 10 years you won't regret that?

I learned from my cousin that life changes, and you can either change with it or get left behind. So why did my cousin announce her sexual orientation at 15 and then at 20 starts dating a man whom she would eventually marry and have children with? As a very close relative, my theory is that she was confused and hurting, and this was a way to escape from the family model she grew up with and did not want to replicate. So she tried to find a way out of what she thought her future as a heterosexual would be.

Do I think my stepson is similar this way? Initially, yes, I thought it was possible he was using this as an excuse or to get attention. Making such an extreme announcement would certainly garner some attention during an extremely tumultuous time in his life. These thoughts came from fear and lack of education.

I no longer believe this after years of research, prayer, and reflection. Now that I have had more experience with people who are not heterosexual, I realize how ignorant and intolerant I was. I can see how wrong my thoughts were. Life as a homosexual or transgender person need not be any more difficult than life as a heterosexual. Granted, research shows that "LGBT people are nearly four times more likely to experience violent victimization than non-LGBT people." These acts of violence are more commonly perpetrated by people known to the victim than by strangers. This violence is perpetrated from fear, ignorance or intolerance.

Many Christians like to point out what they believe the Bible teaches us about not accepting homosexuality or being transgender. When going through these experiences with my cousin and stepson, I did my own research. So many people will simply "drink the Kool-aid," meaning just follow along with someone else's teaching, never asking questions or challenging the teaching or thought leaders.

Christianity's core teaching and most fundamental principle is "The Golden Commandment," which has two parts. First, "You shall love the Lord Your God with all your heart and with all your soul and with all your mind and with all your strength." The second part states, "You shall love your neighbor as yourself" (Mark 12:30–31). Please take note that the verse does not continue to say, "unless someone is doing something you don't like or understand."

After knowing and watching Elliott for the last several years, I feel that he is living the right life for him. For him, life is meant to be lived as a male. He has met a woman who supports and loves him as he is. It is beautiful that he and his wife are in a relationship that makes them both happy. They are building a life together. Isn't that what any parent wants for their children? To be happy.

Do I think some people are born in the wrong body for their brain? It's entirely possible! In the end, each person has to make their own journey and write their own story. Each story is unique, personal, and beautiful in its special ways.

While many would argue there is no simple solution to this age-old problem of sexual orientation and gender dysphoria, I think there is. The solution is to embrace and celebrate those differences between us.

Let's love each other as we would like to be loved. Love with patience, kindness, and honor. Love that doesn't judge that shows mercy, compassion, tolerance. It's important to have tolerance for people similar to ourselves (which is easy), and have tolerance and acceptance for people who are quite different from us in any way. Physically, spiritually, geographically, politically. Accepting others in all these ways is so important in our world, but the differences we see in each other should be nurtured and lauded as beauty.

Chapter 13
Burnt Bridges

"It takes more energy to hold on to toxicity than to let it go." - Jennifer

Yet Another "Surprise"

Christmas is my favorite holiday of all. I love that we celebrate our Savior's birth by finding the right present for our loved ones. My love language is gifts, so it's important to me to give gifts. It also is important to me to receive gifts. To me, love is expressed through giving and receiving, not necessarily through the actual item given.

The last Christmas I celebrated with my intact family was a bit unusual. Oh, we had the usual morning time of all the kids complaining because Tony wouldn't get out of bed. I'm confident he did that on purpose because he knew we wouldn't open presents until he was up. Finally getting Tony out of bed, the kids made their way to the living room, where Santa had filled the stockings and stacked his stash for us all.

There were even some presents I did not recognize, which was exciting for me because that meant gifts for me! (Moms around the world, I know you feel me on this.) As the children were tearing through their gifts, we heard many shouts of thanks and excitement.

When they finished, they remembered that there were two other people in the room, their dad and I. Immediately, they started to bring gifts over to us, demanding we open them. There were beautiful gifts from each of them. They were all teenagers now or older, and could figure out how to go shopping independently. It made for an exciting Christmas morning!

One last gift remained. Brent grinned and said that it was for me. He picked it up and laid it on my lap. It was exceptionally heavy but was a small package. About the size of an Xbox, actually. I felt confident Brent would not get me an Xbox. I was not and never have been a gamer.

I slowly unwrap the gift, savoring the moment that mothers rarely have. That moment when all the attention is on the mother instead of being in the background. Of course, my children all groaned their annoyance with my slowness.

Finally, the item was unwrapped. It was a rather nondescript black box with a handle, almost like a small briefcase. I slid the closure over and opened the case to find a Glock handgun inside.

What In The Hell?

That was my first and only thought. After that, my mind was completely blank. I had not asked for a handgun or truly expressed a desire to own one. There is a great deal of responsibility that comes with ownership of a gun. I wasn't sure I was able to live up to that responsibility.

Seeing the shock on my face, Brent quickly called out, "Surprise!" Yep, I was surprised. In front of the kids, I swiftly melded my reaction into one of enthusiasm. I proclaimed how surprised I was and couldn't wait to go to the gun range.

That part was accurate. I was excited to shoot the pistol as I had not done that before. My parents owned rifles and shotguns when

I younger, and I had shot them on rare occasions. In fact, my mother was given a rifle as a birthday present from her father for her 16th birthday.

A few days after Christmas, I found myself alone with Brent and no children around, so I could ask him why he thought I wanted a gun for Christmas. He said we had talked about it, and he thought it would be a fun surprise. (There is that word again.)

While I agreed we had certainly talked about purchasing a gun, we had not made any particular agreement or plan to do so. I reminded him of my hesitancy due to the heavy responsibility of gun ownership. Eventually, the conversation devolved into an argument, but I had an extra concern this time. He was angry, I was angry, and there was an easily accessible gun in the house.

I dropped the argument and decided not to bring it up again. He clearly didn't understand me or respect my wishes. I had repeatedly been asking for a very different type of gift. For years, I had requested a right-hand ring. I had provided my ring size, emailed hyperlinks to preferred styles, circled pictures from advertisements, and left them conspicuously for him to find.

Yet, when he decided to purchase a gun (ostensibly for me), he chose to ignore my desires and my stated wishes. He decided that his desires and wishes were greater than mine.

This was another straw added to the camel's back that was my marriage. But, how many more straws could land before the proverbial back was broken?

A Life-Altering Decision

On a cold wintry day about a month after that Christmas, I went to the library and looked up books about the psychological effects of divorce on kids. I looked up multiple books and read them while standing right there between the racks. I found books that said staying with your husband is good and why. I found books that said separating is better and why.

But I finally found one book that was a compilation of interviews with adults whose parents divorced and those whose parents should have divorced but didn't. Those adults with divorced parents didn't have much negative to say, really. They said they thought their lives improved for the most part. And, the adult children whose parents should have divorced but did not say they wished their parents had divorced instead of staying together.

Reading these words from the people themselves led me to take one step closer to the actual divorce. Finally, I had evidence that the children would be okay.

What was better? To live as a couple arguing and creating a tense environment for the kids to live in or to live separately and pass the kids and fight between us over custody, child support, etc.? Not too much choice there, really. I never trusted that he would pay me child support and never thought I could come up with the money to pay an attorney.

The work I did for years raising his kids, making his meals, cleaning his house, laundry, bill paying, trying to keep all our shit together. And at times, there was a lot of shit. But, I did it all for the kids to have a family with both parents. I believed it was the right thing to do.

Then, he cheated. He cheated on me after

all the years I had given him of me. The best of me.

I tried for years to forgive him. To make the changes he needed me to make. To make our home an even better environment for him. But, in the end, I just wasn't suitable for him, and I was finally able to admit it.

It Is Time

Late in June 2013, I met Brent at his office to see the new design and then have a date night for the first time in probably years. I decided to use this time to tell him the conclusion I had come to. I was very nervous, my breath was shallow, my heart was racing, my anxiety was off the charts. I parked in the garage, not near his vehicle; I didn't want to walk out together knowing what I was going to say to him.

I entered the office with serious trepidation. He met me at the front and was happy to see me. I remember him that day as being on top of the world. This was his happy place. I felt guilty that I was going to destroy that shortly, but I also knew it must be done.

He showed me around the office with all

the upgrades and changes he had worked on for months with no raise or promotion even though I had repeatedly encouraged him to request one or both. Yet, he was proud of his work.

I knew this, but I also knew I was checked out emotionally. He introduced me to a couple of people who were still there but preparing to leave. We went to his office. I sat in the chair. The office was small—maybe eight feet by six feet. A large window provided a view of the parking garage.

When we got to his office, he sat down in his desk chair and proceeded to check his email. Once done, he asked me where we should go for dinner. So, he hadn't even thought of it. This reminded me that this wasn't so much a "date night" as it was a chance to show off his work.

I hesitated in responding; he finally looked at me. I told him we needed to talk. He said, "About what?" Ignoring, or perhaps just not wanting to see, any signals he should have heard in my voice. I told him, "I want a divorce." I remember saying it very quietly, and he just stared at me. His body was still from shock, but I could see the emotions in his eyes as they slowly began to register the pain, the reality of what I said, and then the anger started to shoot out intensely.

He sat for a long time, just staring at me. Angry. Speechless. Intimidating. Scary. Confused. He finally said something, I do not remember what, but he was angry. I remember the feelings. Fear, uncertainty, hating the angry, loud, mean, hurtful words. He stormed out of the office, leaving me behind, not caring if I were to get locked in.

At the parking garage, we separated into our own cars. He drove recklessly out, squealing tires and screeching through the place. I feared for his safety. Lord knows I had been in the car with him plenty of times when he drove this way, and it felt out of control, like we could crash at any moment.

I drove over to the Starbucks that was in the same office complex. That's as far as I could get before I completely broke down. I ended up calling each of the kids to tell them what happened. I started with Tony for two reasons: first, he's the oldest, and second, out of fear for his dad's safety. I remember telling him what I had told his dad. I will never forget Tony's calmness, compassion, and sadness on the phone. Little did I know how I would crave that calmness and compassion over the next several months, even years.

I remember talking to Peter. He asked me why I would do this. He truly did not understand. I told him, "You don't know your dad like he used to be. You don't know us any way but arguing and fighting because things have been bad for that long." I told him we just couldn't make each other happy anymore and that we hadn't been able to for many years, if ever.

I remember feeling helpless yet powerful. A strange combination to be sure. But I was helpless. Helpless to stop the wrenching pain I had inflicted on Brent, my sons and my daughters. But, powerful in the knowledge in what I was doing, the decision I had made and how I was following through with it. This was the right decision for me. For my health, and ultimately for Brent's, and for our family.

After talking further with Tony and finding out he could not get ahold of his dad, I tried reaching out to Brent's friend Bob for help making sure Brent was safe. Bob was cold, as expected, but took my call and heard my concern. I don't remember all the words said. I think he tried to assure me Brent was fine and that it wasn't my worry anymore because I had asked for a divorce. I ended up calling the police to get an APB on him for safety. I feared he would try to kill himself. He had made comments about doing so before, but always in the heat of an argument, not really anything I truly thought he would do.

Eventually, after hours of concern and worry, he showed up at the house telling us he had driven to the top of the parking garage and been sitting there the whole time.

Telling friends and family

I remember telling my sisters and a friend about this decision pretty quickly after that night. I was counting on my friend to be my main support. Little did I know that just wouldn't happen because she always has her own issues, but I found two very good new friends. As well as bettering my relationships with my sisters, my divorce put me in a new place with my mom.

As a youngster, I had always been close to my mom. I remember telling her I would live with her forever, as many children do. But, as a sexually active teen, I pulled away from her. I was ashamed of my activities but didn't have the strength of the flesh to stop them. The spirit was willing, but my flesh was so very weak—such a true statement for much of my life.

Looking back, I can see that I was being groomed too. My first serious boyfriend, who would become my first husband, slowly built a wedge between my mom and me. I wouldn't realize it until after the divorce.

Once in a counseling session, while reflecting on my relationship with my mom, I stated that she and Brent both wanted to control me. They would fight over who had control. That was inaccurate. My mom could see I was being controlled in a way that only a parent could see. She was trying to extract me from that. But I didn't know it was happening, so I fought her attempts. After the divorce, I realized these things.

When I finally called my parents to tell them about the divorce, my mom said something I will never forget. She said, "I've been waiting 25 years to hear you say that."

That floored me. Stopped me in my tracks. Here I was, having spent so much time being anxious about letting them down by ending my marriage. Something that was never done in our family or our faith. Marriage is for life. Period. No questions asked.

But then she reacted this way. Really? Wow. I was speechless. No words. But, at the same time, I had an intense feeling of relief. I knew absolutely I had made the right choice for myself, my husband, my kids, and the rest of my family. I knew it deep in my soul even if he didn't know it quite yet.

At the end of the marriage, at the time I made the decision, I definitely felt that a power shift occurred—no more power struggle between the two of us. I had taken over and was no longer struggling with him. I was free and open to all the infinite possibilities of life now.

Granted, I had children to care for, but three were adults, and one who nearly was. They were still my children. They needed my strength and quiet calmness. And I'd already gone through all my emotions. For me, it was over. My feelings were all used up. So it made me available to help my kids through this time as much as I could. And as much as they would let me.

Brent and I coexisted in the same house for the next month while making arrangements for our new, separate lives. I was planning my new life, making my own decisions for the first time in my life. Having complete control over everything, including things like how I dressed and what decor I used.

It was an intense, anxious time. I would not recommend it to anyone. We even slept in the same bed for the first week or 10 days, which was strange. I thought he would choose to sleep elsewhere, but he didn't. And neither did I. One day, after another pointless fight over all of it, I moved my things into my daughter's room. She was away most of that summer, so I used her space.

One morning he came barging into the room and grabbed my laptop and other things, claiming they belonged to him. At first, I got distraught, but I quickly realized that's what he wanted. So, I stopped and said, "Okay, if you want or need that, it's fine." I figured I would just buy myself a laptop.

Well, he did that because he was convinced I was using it to cheat on him. Ha! In front of our children, this man who accused me of not wanting enough sex to satisfy him is now worried I'm cheating on him with someone else. He didn't realize his own folly.

Eventually, he gave me back the laptop. And eventually, we moved out, away from one another.

Labor Day

Over the weekend of Labor Day that year, Peter spent the night at his friend's house on Friday night during our separation. I decided to go out and have some fun too. I contacted a new friend I had made and went to his place. We watched a movie, had a few beers, and I stayed overnight.

As I was driving home the following day, I had several anxious text messages and calls from the kids. They all were agitated, losing it, really. Their father threatened to kill himself unless I sat down and talked with him. I had no desire to do this as my feelings were dead, my decision made, we were done. I wasn't looking back. All the attention he had tried to pay to me during the last 2 months was just "too little, too late."

Reluctantly, I called Brent. I remember we argued severely on the phone, and I eventually agreed to let him come to my house. However, I told him he needed to give me an hour. I knew I was 30 minutes out and wanted time to get in and settle before he arrived.

True to form, he did not respect that time frame and what was waiting for me when I arrived. I pulled onto the driveway and grabbed two lawn chairs from the trunk. I made him sit on the driveway because I did not want his negative, narcissistic energy in my safe place.

We sat down facing each other, and he just sat silently staring at me. I could tell he was highly emotional, and it appeared to me he was angry. But I sat, waiting for him to say something. This too was true to form as he would often grow silent during our marriage and just refuse to discuss issues. But now, I had the strength of my convictions that divorce was the right thing to do for us. And the behavior he exhibited by drawing our children into this confirmed to me that I did make the right choice.

He finally started to talk, saying how much he missed me. I don't even remember reacting. I'm sure some people would have said my behavior was cold and harsh during the meeting. While I wouldn't necessarily disagree with them, I would say I had every right to be cold and harsh. Of course, we all think our personal stance is the right one in these situations.

I decided to hear him out. I asked him what it was about me that he missed. He mentioned my cooking, how I kept the house (which I'm sure I scoffed at), and that he missed having me in bed. I remember saying back to him, "You need a cook, a maid, and a whore." Honestly! He didn't say that he missed anything uniquely me. He could hire someone to meet those three needs. It wasn't me he missed, but what I did for him that he missed. After a more circular conversation, he finally got in his car to leave. After sitting in my driveway for quite some time, he eventually left. It wasn't until he had turned the corner at the end of the block that I got up and went inside.

I called the children, told them I had met with their dad, and told them as much as they needed to know about how the conversation went. And I went on with the rest of my day.

Work Incidents

Even moving out didn't stop him from trying to "get me back." The thing he truly did not understand was that he had blown all the chances and opportunities. But I was emotionally checked out for some time, so these things were just annoying and eventually scaring me.

He sent a bouquet of flowers to my office. That little gift of appreciation you always hope you'll get, something special just on a random day. To know he loves you, wants to be with you, loves your life together.

After I moved out, he finally sent that bouquet I'd wanted for years. I had been asking, I mean straight out saying, why don't you send me flowers anymore? I would love to have flowers just because even if they were picked up from the grocery store on the way home. Just something that said you thought of pleasing me, and only me, for a moment.

For years I said this to him. And nothing happened until after I told him I wanted a divorce, moved out of our bedroom, ended the lease on our home, moved all my stuff to a new place, moved into that new place, and had been there for nearly a month!

Then he sends me a bouquet with chocolates and a little teddy bear. Now he's going overboard because he never thought I should be eating chocolates and would criticize me for doing so, to the point where I had to hide what I ate and when. An unfortunate habit I'm still trying to lose.

The receptionist called me up to receive the flowers and was excited when I came up. Upon reading the card, I advised her I was not interested in receiving them and she was welcome to do whatever she wanted with them. She looked at me like I'd grown a third eye. "I'm serious," I told her. "I really do not want them or the chocolates or the bunny. Share them with the team." I asked her who delivered them, and from her description, it sounded like it was my ex.

I reached out to him again, this time asking

him not to come to my place of employment again. I had no desire to speak to him while at work and asked him to respect that as I would do the same for his place of employment.

Apparently, he thought I was joking or that I wouldn't stick to my guns. A few days later, I went to the parking garage at the end of the day to find my car covered with more than 100 yellow sticky notes—inside and out. Each note said something about a dream or goal we'd had, good times we had enjoyed, a hope we shared. On the steering wheel was the pièce de résistance. It said, "I Love You."

Thank goodness I had a co-worker walking out with me because it scared me to have this happen. To know he could get into my car anytime because he still had the key code for it, was very eye-opening and a bit frightening after this incident. At first, I was just stunned and didn't know what to do. Then, it came to me to call the police at some point. I don't know if my co-worker suggested it or if I thought of it, but it sounded like a good idea.

The Cobb County police came and took the report. They suggested getting a restraining order against him. I just didn't know for sure if I should or not. I knew I wanted him to stop but that sounded a bit drastic. Upon further conversation with the police and talking about how these were things Lifetime movies are made of, I agreed it was a good idea and started the process.

Cable Box Catastrophe

Brent called me at work on a random afternoon, saying he needed his cable TV box back immediately. I found that interesting since I'd had it for a few months, and he didn't seem to need it until that day. He didn't have any issue with leaving it in the house we shared and said he had all his stuff out. But, whatever, it's something I wasn't using so he could have it. But I sure didn't want to meet him alone at my house after the last time he came over.

I called Tony, my eldest child, to see if he could and would be willing to meet his dad to give him the cable box. Tony readily agreed, so I made the arrangements with my ex and went about my day. My only stipulation was to meet him outside and not let him in the house. I simply didn't want his energy in that space. It was my place that I had made my very own and was very comfortable in it.

Around the meeting time, I got a frantic call from Tony. He was crying and could barely choke out, "Mom, I'm sorry. I didn't know he was going to do that." I finally settled him down enough to determine he was okay and didn't need immediate help from the authorities. I asked him to take a breath and start at the beginning with what had happened. I truly had no idea or clue what was going on. And I never would have guessed what he was about to say.

Brent told me about arriving at the house and letting himself in. He found the cable box and set it by the front door, ready for his dad to show up.

His dad knocked on the door a short time later. Tony opened the door with the cable box in hand, intending for his dad to take the box and leave, as I had instructed. The next thing he knew, Tony was shoved aside by his own father, who then ran up the stairs to my bedroom.

Tony followed him, telling him he needed to leave, asking what he was doing, begging him to go. He didn't belong there. His dad picked up the laptop I used at the time and dug through my dresser until he found the gun he had given me for Christmas the year before. A gift I had not asked for. This gift said more about him and less about me. We had previously talked about getting a gun but never agreed to it. He just surprised me with one, but really it was more for him than anything else. It was the only gun in the house.

He took the laptop and the gun along with the cable box and left. That's when Tony called me. The poor kid felt so guilty for letting his dad in and was shocked at his dad's behavior. He was barging into someone else's home and stealing their possessions.

I was furious, so angry, angrier than I think I had been up to that point. For him to have done that to our son! The feelings of frustration and rage coursed through me while I searched for the right thing to say to Tony as this was clearly not his fault, even though he felt he had let me down. I finally told Tony that I was not considering this his fault at all in any way, shape, or form. This was beyond his control, and he did all he could to make it better.

After talking to my support crew (my counselor and trusted friends) about it, I ended up filing a police report because I didn't know what else to do. The police told me to try to negotiate for the items to be returned to me and advised they'd be happy to facilitate a meeting to make sure everything went smoothly at an exchange.

So, I started to reach out to him. Of course, at first, he wouldn't even reply. Eventually, I pestered him enough that he answered me. When he finally answered, he agreed to return my things if I met him with no police. I don't recall even telling him about the police conversation, so that was interesting. I told him that I was not willing to forego having someone there to keep the peace and safety. Obviously, we couldn't count on how he would behave since he had taken some of his actions.

After 36 hours of negotiating, we agreed to meet the following day at the Outlet Shoppes of Atlanta. I immediately called the police about it and asked for an escort they assured me they would provide.

The morning of the exchange, I woke as

nervous as a wet bunny on a tightrope above an electric fence the next day. I called on my support crew to get me through this as I had an untold number of times previously. The meeting time approached, so I headed to the meeting spot to talk with the officer beforehand.

When I arrived at the Outlet Shoppes, there were very few people there before opening time. I parked in the large lot behind McDonald's, and the police car pulled up shortly after me. We spoke for a few minutes, and I spotted Brent's car in the McDonald's parking lot. I could just feel him watching. Roaring in as fast as his car would go, he came to a screeching halt directly behind the police car and in front of mine.

He proceeded to whip the car door open and hold his hands up in the air with the gun in one and the computer in the other. The police officer immediately told him to stay in his car, sit still and calm down.

But, true to his nature, he would not listen. He shoved the items at the officer in such a way that he had no choice but to grab them. Spun around, got back in his car, and spun his tires as he flew out of the parking lot. The officer had a few choice words for him, but in the end, we were both glad the exchange had taken place without a serious incident.

Of course, I had concerns about Brent having my computer for 36 hours. I didn't trust Brent at all when it came to the possibility of putting spyware or some kind of tracking software on the machine. I asked Chris, my favorite IT guy at work, to wipe the computer and reload it for me. Luckily, Chris was happy to help and took care of it quickly. He truly understood what I was dealing with since he was there when some of the incidents at work had taken place.

The results were exactly as I had hoped: I had my possessions back, and no one was physically harmed. I was so proud of myself for working through this process calmly and effectively.

Freedom On The Horizon

Once I was free of Brent physically and financially, I could save up a good sum and managed to come up with the money for a lawyer (at a discount, but still). Then, I wrote up the divorce paperwork myself and filed it. If it weren't for the fact that Brent hired an attorney after the gun and computer incident, I never would have. But, once he did it, I felt I had to in order to protect myself. In the end, it was reassuring to know that the lawyer had to keep my best interests, my safety, as his foremost concern.

I had visited Cherokee Women's Shelter a month or so before to find out how to obtain the restraining order. I went back to them now and filed the request with the court. I also asked how to hire an attorney and get some sort of discount since I had all the paperwork completed and filed.

They referred me to a lawyer in Canton who worked out an arrangement for me, and then, once he realized how much work I did, he lowered it even more. He contacted my ex's attorney and started working out details. Brent kept harassing me with obnoxious emails and texts, commenting on how unfair the settlement was. And he was right. It was unfair. I was taking the burden of the debts myself and not asking for any child support even though I would have our youngest child the majority of the time. But that's not how he saw it.

My attorney worked back and forth with him. The last straw was when we had everything worked out, my ex added that he now wanted me to pay pet support and for pet bills since he now had both dogs.

Not Gonna Happen

My attorney pushed back hard, and they finally finished the process. They wrapped up the negotiations, and then, when I got his final bill, he had lowered it even more. I'm pretty sure that was his way of helping me after 23 years with this "tool," as he called Brent.

The paperwork was initially filed on October 17 (my birthday) and was finalized, signed by the judge on December 17 (my dad's birthday), a mere two months later. Mostly because we had no assets to fight over, and I had agreed to take the bulk of the debt, there wasn't too much hassle.

It was done.

Chapter 14

Becoming Me

"Expect beauty in life, even in the unexpected."
- Jennifer

In many ways, recounting all these incidents is more complicated than going through it the first time in real life. However, writing it down and committing it to the ages has reaffirmed the reality of what happened. All that happened will always be a part of my story.

But, these experiences do not define me nor determine my worth.

I buoy my courage to continue by remembering that this is all done in the spirit of the "so that" principle. I am sharing my experiences, reflections, and results hoping that others who experience similar situations will find it helpful.

You must know that YOU are valuable. You must know that you are worthy of being more than you are right now, wanting more than you have, expecting more positive experiences in life. I have done the work of experiencing these feelings again to get that message to you. It is too important that you know you are loved and worthy of that love for me to hold back.

The decision to divorce was the single most difficult decision I ever had to make in my life. I don't remember struggling that much when I found out I was pregnant with my first child. Then, of course, I was much younger, and much more naive.

This time, I knew the fallout of this decision would forever alter so many lives of people I loved in negative ways. Knowing this made the decision harder, but it also convinced me that it was the only way Brent or I could truly be happy. As his wife, I was unable to fulfill his needs. Since I had finally admitted this to myself, I also knew I would never be able to satisfy him as a life partner.

I took this decision very seriously. I spent years in contemplation, prayer, journaling, researching, discovering, and exploring. I slept on it for weeks to ensure I had no remorse about the choice.

Brent and I talked about retiring at the beach for many years. We talked about what that looked like for each of us, and I had a picture for that. That picture, and the pain it caused to think it would never happen, is what stopped me from divorcing sooner. But when that picture started to fade and turn bleak, gray, and cold, I knew it was time.

Once I decided that it was the right decision, I started to see a new picture of the future as a divorced woman. I could now see the future in bright possibilities instead of bleak and gray. Granted, the picture was very different. I was alone, but I enjoyed my life on the beach. Happy, loved, and wholly myself.

The only anxiety I felt about the choice was telling Brent, but no longer with the choice itself.

I can only attribute this to truly becoming me and listening to my own needs. I know that God was in this decision because I invited Him in through my journaling, prayers, meditation, and dreaming. I know that as much as God hates divorce, He hates to see His children suffer even more.

In fact, since the divorce, I've had a lot of time to contemplate the institution of marriage. Is our society's version of marriage the version God truly intended or has humankind altered it? There are so many beautiful things God put in place that humans have perverted that it wouldn't surprise me to find out that was the case.

The biggest reason I knew that divorce was the right decision was that there was no way I would ever have my own emotional or physical needs met by Brent. As I said before, I also knew that he would not be fulfilled by what I could provide for his needs.

During the contemplation of divorce, when journaling, I would often write out my needs. I did this as part of relearning myself and allowing me to be my real self. Listing out my needs and how so many of them were not met led me to conclude that I would be better off not married than married.

I also wrote out what I understood to be Brent's needs. Obviously, I already knew the biggest one - our physical relationship. I kept going further with all I could come up with. I realized, again, that I was not going to be able to meet his needs. I knew that both of us would have a better chance at happiness if we could just get out of each other's way.

Once the divorce was finalized, I felt such a sense of relief. I remember feeling like I could catch a full, deep breath for the first time in over 23 years. The sense of freedom and possibility for the future was so strong it was nearly overwhelming.

I was becoming my true self and ready to explore all the possibilities.

Chapter 15
A Match Made Online

"Don't cheat on the future by living in the past."
- Jennifer

Dating

After a time of living separated and then divorced, I thought I was ready to explore dating again. Dating was a new experience for me. Brent and I started dating at 15 (sorry Mom), married at 19, and now, I was 41. I'd never really dated much. I went out with a boy a time or two in high school, but that was it.

Does that even count?

Now is my time to have fun and explore what I like in a man! I knew I had to kiss a few frogs before I found my future husband.

I started an account online, and I got some interest. It was cool to see guys want me. It sends a rush every time a new guy sent you a message- even if you didn't like them. It just felt like a nice compliment to feel wanted.

Dating taught me a lot about social norms.

For example, I had no idea what a booty call was. Boy, that was a shocker- I had to tell one date to leave right away after he showed up at my door. It was just a strong no. But I was now empowered to say no as well.

I don't think it's necessary to get into all my post-divorce dating adventures. So many were of the sort that using "adventure" to describe them would be a complete overstatement. However, I do have some lessons learned, so I intend to describe only what is needed for those lessons to be relayed—no need to describe anything salacious, as if.

I dated one man, Walt, for several months, but in the end, I broke it off because I felt we were just too different. I felt my kids would never respect him as my choice of mate, which would affect how I saw him. Truly, it was already affecting my view of him. So I broke up with him.

Months went by, during which I occasionally dated here and there, but nothing too serious. I kept thinking of Walt. I couldn't seem to get past him. I thought about him all the time. I remember thinking at one point, "Satan, get behind me, quit putting these thoughts in my head." No matter what I did, I couldn't seem to get past him though. Finally, I discussed my thoughts and feelings with my most trusted girlfriends, and it seemed like the best choice was to call him up and see if he still thought about me. Nothing ventured, nothing gained.

I texted Walt, and surprisingly he responded quickly. He said he had not been able to stop thinking of me either. So we texted quite a bit that first night and eventually made a plan to meet. I can still remember that feeling of giddiness, that childlike joy, of seeing him again after all these months.

We started dating again, and I told my kids I was seeing him. I told myself that this was my life and my choice, no matter what my kids thought. We started talking about the future. He had been shopping for a house to buy, and now I joined him in that search. We moved very quickly, way too quickly.

I found myself compromising again. Acquiescing to whatever I thought he would be most amenable to. He did the same. Neither of us was happy because we were both compromising so much. We were reacting to the situation with desperation, really. We each were worried about being alone, and therefore we did what we could to avoid that. Loneliness, or the fear of it, is the worst reason in the world to be with someone.

Our relationship became so serious that I convinced myself to move 30 miles away from my children. After a couple of months of living together it started to fall apart.

The relationship had crumbled to the point that I didn't even recognize it. I didn't know how to get out of it. I didn't have the courage or conviction to do so. The walls started caving in around me and I felt there was just no way to right the turns I had taken on my current "adventure". It was just life and me exploring how to date again. I felt so discouraged and sad that I cried, desperately, the entire way home after work one night.

When I got home, I went straight to bed and cried most of the night. Understandably, Walt was highly concerned and tried to help in the best way he could. He encouraged me to go to the hospital as he feared I would find a way to harm myself.

I remember telling him I was glad I had sold my gun because I was afraid I would use it on myself if I had it. Now I know I would never do that to myself or my children, grandchildren, and family. But I can certainly see how that scared him so badly that night. Honestly, it scared me to feel that way and so intensely that I voiced my feelings.

My visit to the hospital eventually led to a brief stay at a private psychiatric hospital. During those few days in the psych hospital, my biggest fear was missing my daughter's college graduation, but I did safely make it in time.

While staying at the hospital, I asked my sons to pack my things from the home I had been living in with Walt to not have to go back again. He did what he thought was best in the situation, but he was not truly in love with me any more than I was with him. Upon my release, I went to my son's home and eventually found my footing and a better path for my life.

This may seem extreme, and you may even think that there's no way you would get to that point. But I guarantee you. I never thought

I would either! It was a series of small choices, one after another, that built on each other and locked me into a situation from which I couldn't extract myself.

A New Start

After staying with my eldest son and his wife for a few months, I stabilized my emotions and saved enough money to work on finding a new home for myself. I decided it needed to be affordable enough that I could pay the rent with unemployment compensation and still afford my car. In addition, I realized I needed to be able to completely and fully take care of myself. I had always had some sort of partner. Now it was truly on me, and I finally acknowledged this to myself.

In February of 2016, I moved into a 2-bedroom, 1.5-bath mobile home on Main Street in Kennesaw. That first night was the hardest night of my life. I had never lived alone before. Even through the separation and divorce, I lived with my youngest son and daughter. Yet, here I was at 44, doing so for the first time.

So many things in my life were not the way

I planned them to be. But that's kind of how my life had always been. I've not been a big planner per se. I never felt settled enough to do so. I don't know if that was because of the marriage issues or just my personality.

I found myself sitting alone in the living room of my new home. Cold and exhausted after a long day of moving in. There were soft spots and holes in the floor where the only thing keeping it from falling through was the carpet. I'd already found several dead bugs to clean up, and the windowsills were coated with black dirt, which I just prayed wasn't mold.

There was no microwave in the place, and you could not open the oven door more than about halfway because it would hit the fridge's handle. I probably wouldn't be baking or cooking much anyway because I didn't know how to cook for just one person.

The last time I cooked for one or two people was more than 25 years ago. We were just starting out, and we had little money. It was easy to cook small, simple meals. Through the years, I've cooked for six people and more regularly. I enjoyed entertaining and cooking, but that wouldn't be happening in this tiny place.

The moving-in process was much easier on this move than so many others because, over the past 3 ½ years, I had purged so many belongings in the moves. I just hoped I wouldn't wish for some of those things back. My kids teased me for keeping so many things through the years. Just wait until they have kids and want to see or even use some of those things. Then they'll be happy I kept some of them. Let's be honest though, it's more complaining from the boys who wouldn't care about the sentimental things as much as the girls anyway.

The first night was the hardest. I cried myself to sleep. I stayed up much later than I probably should have in an attempt to avoid going to bed alone. The day had been emotional and exhausting. I certainly didn't do myself any favors by stalling bedtime. I was scared, though.

Being the first time I had truly lived alone was frightening at this point in my life. I sobbed so hard that night. The feeling of being all alone in the world was intense. I knew intellectually I was not alone, but my feelings told me otherwise. This was the first time I consciously realized that my feelings would lie to me.

The following day, when I woke up, I was determined to make a good start.

Turning on the shower, I let the water warm up while looking through my clothes. A short time later, I got in the shower. Before I could even shampoo my hair, the water suddenly became freezing. So shockingly cold! I adjusted the dials, trying desperately to get some heat. No luck at all. Not one drop of warmth was coming out of the faucet. Finally, I gave up, climbed out of the shower, and, as I toweled off, the tears started to flow. Here I was, day one of my new life, and I couldn't even get a hot shower! How was I possibly going to take care of myself?

I had to work that day, so I used extra deodorant and perfume to cover the dust and grime from moving. Dry shampoo was caked in my hair to stop the greasy sheen. I made it through the day, but it was another tough one.

I cried again as I went to bed that night, but it was not quite as long or as hard. Each day, I survived a bit easier. I figured out the tiny water heater tank by not running hot water first. Turn it on and jump in! Some lessons are quicker to learn than others.

As I moved into this new place physically, I found myself in a new place emotionally as well. I purposely chose this rental because I knew that I could still pay the rent with the unemployment funds even if I found myself unemployed. I could also save some money for emergencies due to the low rent. I could survive financially on my own here. I had the ways and means to do so.

The next item to work on would be me. I needed to learn who I was at my very core as opposed to following the most recent emotion flitting through my atmosphere. Living alone allowed for more quiet time, reflection, prayer, thoughts than I had ever allowed or experienced before. That was the truly scary part for me. It wasn't so much being physically alone as it was being emotionally alone.

One man I dated told me that he had learned years ago that each of us must first be comfortable with ourselves before we can be comfortable sharing ourselves with others. At the time, I remember thinking that it made sense. But now, in my quiet little home, I could truly find out if I was comfortable keeping my own silence. I was not.

I decided that I needed to take a good amount of time, at least 6 months, maybe a year or more, to just be me. I needed to learn what I was about, what I truly liked, believed, and desired. I remember thinking I should experience all the seasons and holidays on my own before trying to venture into any kind of romantic relationship.

After 10 months of learning to love who I was and finding ways to move forward in my life, I felt truly ready to explore the possibility of finding a mate. Not just dating to date, but actually finding a mate. I had been praying about it for some time and continued to do so. I really wanted God to find the right person for me, not just any person who I could find, since my choices were not always the best. But God's decisions are always wise.

During this time, God spoke to me in dreams about my mate. He told me that He was preparing a mate for me just the same as I was being prepared. That created such excitement in me. The same excitement I believed I would feel upon meeting this special person.

I signed up for an exclusive online dating service for professional adults. After a few weeks on the service, and getting lots of weird messages from men old enough to be my dad or grandpa, I decided to take control.

I read a profile for a beautiful human with a romantic soul and a mischievous grin. I decided to reach out to him. I think it was an important step for me to initiate communication. I truly felt in control of myself and my boundaries were respected during this process.

We texted and talked on the phone for three weeks before meeting in person. Whenever I think of that first meeting and how I felt watching him walk down the sidewalk toward me, I get goosebumps all over again. My feelings of excitement have not wavered to this day.

I met the man who is today my husband.

Nothing in this relationship was pushed or forced. I have maintained my sense of self and held to my ideals. There is no call for me to compromise on my strong beliefs and ideals because my husband shares them. God truly prepared us for each other.

As a faithful child of God, I was in tune enough with Him to know when to act and when to be still.

Chapter 16
Becoming Whole

"The two most important days in your life are the day you were born and the day you find out why."
- Mark Twain

Be Kind to Yourself.

Freedom. Sometimes you don't even realize it is missing until you have it again. For me, freedom was like a new world, and I was addicted to it.

I finally got to explore freedom at the end of my marriage. Freedom gave me new knowledge about myself and what I wanted. I got to discover quite a bit about myself. Most notably was the metamorphosis I would go through each time I dated someone. With each new date, I found myself aligning my thoughts and beliefs with the guy. After doing so for about the fourth time, I realized that I was not staying true to myself but was changing with the wind. I was so disappointed in myself.

I knew I had to do something differently.

Which meant I had to stop dating. I promised myself I would not date anyone until I knew my core values and beliefs and could stand in my own conviction.

It took several months of soul searching to figure this out and embed these values in my heart and soul. Praying, journaling, counseling, women's bible study group, and my own time of reflection helped me to feel comfortable with myself. I was so far from being comfortable in my own skin that I couldn't even let my guard down when I was alone.

I didn't know who I was. I wondered if I ever really did know myself before taking this timeout. Not genuinely knowing myself is why I ended up at rock bottom. I had compromised so much for the man I was with that I wasn't me anymore. I didn't recognize myself. I didn't know how to find myself. I thought all hope was lost. That's why I wanted to end my life. It seemed the simplest solution.

But the beauty of life is seldom found in the simplest solutions. More often, the true beauty of life is found in the moments at rock bottom as we start to climb back up again. Those times in life when we triumph over disappointment or shame are the ones most glorious.

I learned a lot from each relationship - my marriage and dating. The most important thing I learned is that my kids and grandkids are more important to me than any other humans on the earth. I relearned that God gives us infinite chances to live in a way that is pleasing to Him. I learned that love could be fickle, that compromising everything about myself is not love, and that caring about another person's happiness is not good enough to change your entire life.

When these revelations occurred, I had been a mom for 25 years. I had dedicated my time, talents, and resources completely and wholly to my kids' growth and well-being. So why was I changing all that for this one person? I realized that the "right" person wouldn't require that of me. I am grateful every day that God stepped in and saved me from myself at this moment. I have so much life to live and love to give and joy to experience, and sorrow to share with others, but I got lost inside my misery.

Please do NOT hold back these feelings of sorrow and shame. Instead, express them and keep talking about them until you find a way past them or someone to help with them. If you ever feel completely at the end of your own strength or ability, please reach out to a suicide prevention hotline, friend, neighbor, Uber driver, co-worker, or anyone at all.

Please don't be fooled. I did not become whole because I found a man to share my life with—quite the opposite. I became whole by listening to myself and my needs. I became whole by honoring myself, by learning about myself in a way I hadn't done for years. After I learned to honor myself, then I considered sharing my life with a man.

When I ended my first marriage, I was setting the first boundary for myself without realizing it. A boundary that announced I would take no more of the mental abuse, intimidation, or belittling. A boundary that said I know I am worthy of being treated with respect and love.

Setting boundaries is vitally important to your well-being. Just as you would set boundaries for your own moral compass- no lying, cheating, stealing, or a physical boundary - do not put hands on others in anger; you must demand that others respect your boundaries. You must value yourself enough to set and keep the boundaries that will keep you healthy and happy. Having boundaries and enforcing them is empowering.

If you go outside of those boundaries, the typical feeling is disappointment, even disgust. By staying within those boundaries, your own strength continues to rise to the point of invincibility.

Be Humble and Kind

The phrase "always be humble and kind" is a great example of a simple boundary to establish. By humbling ourselves to receive love and be comforted, we can then share that kindness with others. Being kind is a choice we make to positively and purposefully impact our little corner of the world.

Please note, though, being humble does not mean you are a doormat. It means that you are not aggressive, you are respectful, you can walk away when that's the right thing to do.

Be kind to yourself

Please go back and read these words carefully and then reread them. Pace your breathing as you read these words, draw them into yourself. Feel how important you are first and foremost. Repeat this to yourself daily. Say it out loud any chance you get. Write it on cards or sticky notes and use them in your house, your car, your office. Make it a background on your phone.

Whatever you are currently going through, whatever you have gone through in the past, whatever you will walk through in the future, these situations are all meant to be used to draw comfort from God. Once we receive that comfort, we need to share that comfort with others.

When we see that mom whose child seems out of control in the store, instead of glaring at her, maybe a nice smile would be more kind. We've all experienced a moment of great shame or embarrassment. Extend the grace you wish you had received to that mom who needs it. The "so that" principle tells us that God will provide comfort in our time of need so that we can share that same comfort with others.

God uses every experience we have for good and to glorify His plan. Nothing we do, say, or think can separate us from His love. Nothing that isn't already in His plan will stand the test of time. Nothing that is in His plan can be stopped. He yearns for us to love one another, be kind to one another and share joy.

So often, when bad things happen in our lives or to our loved ones, we want to know why. But, there isn't always a reason. Sometimes it just is.

Sometimes the reason is to experience the comfort and mercy of God to share that same comfort and mercy with someone who needs it. That could happen the next day or the next decade, but if you are looking for a chance to share love and kindness, you will find it.

The "so that" principle will bring you comfort and mercy to heal yourself so that you can pass that same comfort and mercy to whoever needs it. This is your purpose. This is the purpose we all share.

Your "So That" Story

As you've read my experiences and "so that" moments, you may have had several "aha" moments concerning events in your own life. I would love to hear from you and to encourage you.

Join our online community to connect with others who also have had "so that" experiences. Share your moments with other like-minded individuals to encourage them.

Join here:
www.facebook.com/groups/growth.comm

Or through my website:
www.jenniferandersensmith.com

Thank You

Thank you so much for sharing in my journey. I hope that you found a nugget of inspiration or wisdom that you can carry with you as you move through life.

I would love to hear from you directly about how this book impacted you. It would be very helpful for myself and for others who could benefit from the book.

If you are willing to share your comments publicly, please leave a review on the website where you purchased the book. If you prefer to share your comments in private, you can contact me through my website, *www.jenniferandersensmith.com*.

Lightning Source UK Ltd.
Milton Keynes UK
UKHW022036260522
403595UK00003B/117